DATE DUE

Oct	19	04	

LUTHER AND MUSIC

LUTHER

AND

MUSIC

DISCARDED

by
PAUL NETTL

Translated by FRIDA BEST and RALPH WOOD

NEW YORK / RUSSELL & RUSSELL

Reprinted from a copy in the collections of
The New York Public Library

FOREWORD

This book attempts a survey of Luther's relation to music and gives a short outline of evangelical church music with a consideration of contemporary theological and religious movements. My most important sources are the philosophical writings of Wilhelm Dilthey, the theological and historical works of Hans Preuss, and the musicological books of H. J. Moser, Rudolph Steglich, Hermann Abert, and Friedrich Blume, to whose *History of Evangelical Church Music* I am particularly indebted.

I wish to thank the following persons whose general helpfulness made it possible for me to write and publish this book: Dr. Else Staudinger, the Rev. Frederic Forell, Else Maria Dane, Professor Otto Piper, Dr. Luther D. Reed, Raymond Brandes, and Mrs. Margaret Bush, my untiring secretary. My deepest gratitude I must express to my friends, Dr. Ralph Wood and Mrs. Frida Best, who share the responsibility for the English version of this work.

PAUL NETTL

CONTENTS

CHAPTER ONE

LUTHER'S PERSONAL RELATION TO MUSIC

During the seventeenth century the musical leadership of Europe shifted from Italy to Germany. This change must be ascribed to Protestantism. The mighty growth of music, culminated by the creative work of Johann Sebastian Bach, can be explained neither by the political history of the Germans nor by their philosophy. It was rather the result of the Lutheran Reformation and of the various religious movements following in its wake. And there are weighty reasons why Protestantism rather than the Catholic Counter-Reformation movement brought about this great florescence of music.

"Roman Catholic piety," writes Oswald Spengler in *The Decline of the West*, "expresses itself in the altarpiece, while Protestant piety is represented in the oratorio. The Isenheim Altar and Bach's St. Matthew Passion are the high lights of these two evolutionary phases." And Thode, in the Munich edition of Luther, says: "The primary role formerly played by painting was now taken over by music."

It would seem that the genius of music had its wings clipped during the Middle Ages. The religious feeling

1

of the Gothic age is embodied in its architecture and painting, while its music is comparatively primitive. Even Palestrina, in whose works piety finds most profound expression, seems devoid of significance when placed next to Bach. The art of tones has been proven a uniquely Protestant art. Protestant piety has found best artistic expression in music. The jubilant faith of Luther, his joyful experience of God, his teaching of salvation by grace, caused him to break out in exultation before his God, and his feelings could find expression only in music.

MUSIC IN THE CATHOLIC CHURCH

Catholic church music interprets religious experience quite differently. True enough, the motets and masses of the Middle Ages breathe a deeply religious spirit; but they are vocal and instrumental adaptations of a melody already existent (tenor). As such they represent a collectivistic feeling. The composer as well as the listener is completely dominated by the ideological power of the church. In a Kyrie or Gloria by Dufay or Binchois, not even the simple melody which runs through the mass is the composer's own. It is something that has come to him not from within, but from without. It may have been taken from a Gregorian chant, or from a well-known folk song. The various voices imitating one another in canonical form reflect the single-mindedness of a religious community, spiritually united or, rather, dominated by the idea of the omnipotence of *Una Sancta Catholica Ecclesia*.

The mass of Palestrina, together with the Gregorian Mass, represents Catholic church music in its purest, most perfect form. World and eternity seem to be merged in perfect harmony. The melody, as the expression of a personal mood, subsides; the rhythm expresses no personal will. It is like a solemn procession, in which the individual voices are merged into an exalted whole, and the stream of harmony flows along in even measure. The dissonances are resolved so gently that the eternal harmony seems in no wise disturbed. There is no contrast between loud and soft, between light and shade, to disturb its supernatural serenity, nor does the sensuous charm of sharply accentuating instruments dispel the beauty of this music.

How different is the effect of Bach's music, where every note breathes the spirit of redemption and grace and of personal relation to God!

The objective piety of the Middle Ages has given way to an eminently subjective one — salvation by faith. Here grace, devotion, comfort, and joy are personally experienced, and find their expression in music that stems from the innermost heart of man. Bach's melodies reflect his personal experiences. For Bach, like Luther, received his inspiration from the Bible with its impressive pictorial language, and he approached his God without the mediation of the Church. The Christian, as Luther sees him, accepts the Word of God as his only standard of faith and life. His faith is founded directly on the Word of God. This excludes pontifical mediation from without, and sets up a universal priesthood embracing all believers. The old hierarchic idea of the Church is set aside. To Luther the Church is an invisible communion of believers. Its only function is to proclaim the Word of God, and to administer the Sacraments. Thus religion is freed from clerical domination and the way is open for a personal experience of God. It is implanted in the soul of man, whence it can blossom in beauty, as it does in the music of J. S. Bach.

The old Church divided Christendom into three distinct groups: priests, believers, and catechumens. This tripartition was applied in a musical sense as well: the soloist who carried out the Gregorian chant, the artistically trained choir of the *Ministri*, and the simple song of the congregation — the latter more or less tolerated as a necessary evil. The Reformation, with its emphasis on the priesthood of all believers, brought about a change in the music of the church service. Congregational singing in unison began to take the leading part. Those musically trained formed a motet chorus, while the minister chanting at the altar was but the representative of the congregation.

MUSIC IN THE REFORMED CHURCH

While Calvinism threw overboard all religious music and retained only congregational singing in unison, Luther never discarded the old musical liturgy entirely. Iconoclastic Calvinists and Zwinglians on the other hand were opposed to artistic expression in any form. Zwingli, the Swiss reformer, in spite of his musical talent (he set two of his own songs to four-part music, and played almost every instrument), cold-bloodedly allowed the organ in Zurich to be hacked to pieces, while the organist stood by, helpless and weeping. Calvin, as well as Zwingli, feared that music would distract the believers from the true purpose of religion. Fanatics in Switzerland stormed the churches and monasteries, destroyed the altar paintings, statues, and organs. The famous organist Hans Kotter, in Berne, was forced to give up his profession and become a schoolmaster. No organ was allowed to be played in Heidelberg from 1570 to 1657. In the hymnbook of the Bohemian Brothers, Katharina Zell fulminated against the senseless "cradle rocking on the organ," by which she meant the old Christmas carols, such as *Joseph, lieber Joseph mein* ("Joseph, Dearest Joseph Mine") and others that delight us even today.

In 1571 two fanatics broke into the church in Frankfort on the Main and seized the organ. In 1563 the organist Candius Sebastiani had been forced to write a defense of this musical instrument.

The vandalism perpetrated by these fanatics is doubtless to be condemned from the theological as well as from the artistic standpoint. But we must not forget that until well into the seventeenth century the masses of the old Church made use of French, Italian, and German folk songs which were often of a lascivious nature and in no wise adapted to arouse religious thoughts and feelings. Songs like *L'homme Armé, Se la face est pale, la cause est amer, Puisque l'amour m'a pris en déplaisir, L'ami de Madame,* and *Rosa Bella* are some of the favorite melodies used in the masses of Dufay, Josquin, Palestrina, and even Monteverdi. However, the Calvinists and Zwinglians went to inexcusable extremes. Many documents of Luther's day condemn these puritanical tendencies. Thus Johann Ott, in his famous song collection of 1544, warns "not to exclude music from the services, as the uncouth jackasses, Anabaptists, and other religious enthusiasts (*Schwaermer*) are doing." And as late as 1627, Pastor Leyser, in his preface to Johann Hermann Schein's *Canzional* thunders against "the Calvinist know-it-alls, who will not tolerate psalteries, harps, organs, and pipes."

We therefore have three conceptions of church music. The strictest and most hostile to art is that of the Calvinists, Zwinglians, and Anabaptists. Their indignation is aroused by the Catholic church ceremonial with its sumptuous pomp, its colorful choral brilliance, its palling ecclesiastical concerts, its overpowering incense swinging — all designed to dull reason and consciousness and to keep the faithful tense with dark mysterious emotions. Between these two extremes we have the Lutheran conception with its emphasis on music as the expression of faith. According to this view, music is a gift of God. God did not create it for the pipers or the dance floors alone, but for a vehicle of prayer and praise.

EARLY INFLUENCES ON LUTHER

Fortunately the ideas of Luther, and not those of Calvin or Zwingli, determined the development of music. Otherwise, we would know nothing of that splendid succession of cantors and organists from which arose the great Bach family. Possibly Germany, too, would have suffered that vacuum in music which so vitally affected Puritan England, and which countries like Switzerland have never quite overcome. That music, nurtured by German Protestantism, throve as it did was due to Martin Luther. His appreciation for the liturgical heritage of the Church and his extraordinary love of music paved the way for a glorious musical tradition. Music has always been a tradition with the people of Thuringia, the German province where Luther's family lived. Wolfram von Eschenbach, the great Minnesinger of the Middle Ages, often alludes to the Thuringians' delight in music. It is a well-known fact that racially mixed populations furnish the best soil for superior musical development; and Saxony-Thuringia, with its mixture of German and Wendish blood, was the homeland of both Handel and Bach. Without doubt musical blood coursed through the veins of Luther's forefathers. Of his mother we know that she loved to sing; the little song, *Mir und Dir ist Niemand huld, das ist unser eigene Schuld* ("No one loves either you or me, but that is the fault of you and me"), that she was in the habit of singing, lived long in his memory. The miners of the county of Mansfeld, a region rich in ore, excelled in song. The *Berg*

Reihen (mountain songs) went from mouth to mouth through the whole country and these "ore diggers" were in great demand as singers. Songs like "Eulogy of Saxon Mines," which is to be found in Rhaw's collection of 1545, were probably well known to Luther; and we find reminiscences of them in Luther's famous battle hymn. Among these songs were such gay tunes as the *Martin's Lieder* then in vogue at Eisleben. *Martin, lieber Herre, lass uns fröhlich sein* ("Martin, dear master, let us be gay") was one of the favorite rounds and was called a *Radel* (wheel).

Perhaps it was not a mere coincidence that the parents gave their son the name of the gay Saint Martin. The lad was well prepared to become a *Kurrende* singer in Eisenach. These singers were mostly young lads who, under the leadership of a prefect, went from house to house (therefore the name *Kurrende*, which is derived from the Latin *currere*, "to run") and sang at the weddings and funerals of rich burghers for a small stipend. *Parteken Hengst* (Alms Horse) was the nickname applied to these boys. And such a one was Martin. We can see him, wearing a black cape and a funny little top hat. Though cold and hungry, he is singing the praise of the Lord, his young heart full of gratitude to his Creator, who had blessed him with a fine voice and a great love for music. These lads suffered much abuse and even blows from the prefect and the rough peasants in the countryside for whom they often sang. And so intimidated were they that once, hearing the gruff voice of a peasant, they took to their heels, although he only meant to give them a few sausages for their fine singing. In later years Luther often remembered these experiences of his boyhood days. "Do not look down on these lads," he said; "I was once one of them. They are not the worst, these little fellows, who go around in patched coats and shoes, and have to earn their bread from door to door. They often become the best, most learned, and famous men. Therefore don't be discouraged, lads, a great good fortune may be in store for you, of which you dream not. Meanwhile do your duty!"

In these years, between 1497 and 1505, Luther may have had access to the works of the great Netherlands masters, Okeghem, Isaak, and Obrecht, or of the Germans, Heinrich Finck and Adam de Fulda. The peasants for whom the *Kurrende* sang did not appreciate these masters. Their art was properly valued rather by the cantors, the rich burghers, and the professors. Simple songs, mostly folk songs, were more to the peasants' liking, and these, too, were part of the excellent repertoire of the *Kurrende*. Luther often recalled the Christmas songs which he sang with his young companions. *Jesu Nate in Bethlehem* ("Jesus, Born in Bethlehem") was the song he loved most. In his lectures on the epistle to the Hebrews, he mentioned the Christmas hymn *Eia Recolamus* ("Let Us Worship").

In his old age, he insisted that people should kneel at the words of the Creed, *Et homo factus est* ("And became man") and intone them solemnly and slowly, "hearing with glad hearts that the Divine Majesty had humbled himself thus far." A special favorite of his was the Christmas hymn:

> *Ein Kindlein so löblich*
> *Ist uns geboren heut'*
> *Von einer Jungfrau säuberlich*
> *Zu Trost uns armen Leut;*
> *Wär' uns das Kindlein nicht geboren*
> *So wären wir allzumal verloren.*

> An infant we worship
> Born to us this day
> Of Virgin Immaculate
> For us poor folk to pray;
> Were us this child not born
> Our souls were helplessly forlorn.

In this hymn he found nothing lacking which would convey the true spirit of Christmas. And he may have valued the tune as highly as that of *Komm Heiliger Geist* ("Come, Holy Ghost") which he believed inspired by the Holy Ghost himself. Of the Easter hymn "Christ is Arisen," which he dearly loved, he said, "Whoever wrote it must have had good judgment, for after a time one tires of singing all other hymns. But the 'Christ is Arisen' one can always sing again."

Luther's deeply religious but Faust-like mentality had aroused in him the desire to become a monk, although as a student he enjoyed good times, songs, dances, and the companionship of congenial men and women. In the summer of 1505 he narrowly escaped death when lightning struck a tree close to him. Then and there he made the irrevocable vow to enter the Augustinian monastery in Erfurt. The history of his doubts and self-castigations is well known. From the musical point of view it must be stressed that, as a priest celebrating the Gregorian Mass, he became well acquainted with the music of the Church.

The journey to Rome, undertaken in a matter concerning his Order, proved most significant for both his theological and his musical development. It was there that the gross worldliness of the papacy came to his attention. It was there that for the first time he breathed the atmosphere of great European music as represented by Josquin des Prés. Josquin, born about 1450, had been in Milan, Ferrara, and Rome since 1484 and is supposed to have spent some time in Paris at the court of Louis XII. Finally he returned to his homeland, where he was provost of the Cathedral Chapter in Condé until his death in 1521. The clear-cut classical style as evinced in his motets and masses — partly vocal and partly instrumental — proves him without equal among his contemporaries. Perhaps Luther came into personal contact with Josquin; and certainly he heard many of his compositions. From that time on, Josquin was always his favorite composer. Once, after a rendition of one of Josquin's beautiful motets, when there had been great general applause, Luther sighed, "Alas, how many fine musicians have died within these past ten years!" and he mentioned Josquin as the greatest of these.

LUTHER'S LOVE OF MUSIC

When Luther entered his great struggle on October 31, 1517, by posting his famous Ninety-five Theses on the portals of the Wittenberg church, music became the sweet comforter of his bitterest hours — his solace, inspiration, joy, and balm. "Music is a beautiful, gracious gift of God. It has often been the inspiration of my sermons," he writes in his *Encomium Musices* ("Eulogy of Music"). "Music rouses all the emotions of the human heart; nothing on earth is so well suited to make the sad merry, the merry sad, to give courage to the despairing, to make the proud humble, to lessen envy and hate, as music." Luther himself played the lute and the flute, and he had a soft, tenor voice, which served him well when he and his friends sang the works of the Flemish and German masters. From student days on, the lute was always his favorite instrument. When in 1521 he made his fateful journey to Worms, where the imperial ban was laid upon him, he took his lute, and from it he sought and found great comfort. His bitter enemy, Cochlaeus, at that time dean of the *Liebfrauenstift*, mockingly tells how Luther played the lute at an inn, and how all eyes were turned on him — "this Orpheus in the garb of a monk, and with a tonsure." His narrow-minded enemies could not or would not understand his unfeigned delight in music.

Luther's love of music aroused deep suspicion in the mind of the Rothenburg schoolmaster, Ickelsamer. He relates that a menial from Leipzig had said that he did not think much of Luther, for he could, it is true, play the lute, but he wore shirts with ribbons, and that was not worthy of a true Christian, "who should wear a gray frock." Emser, another of his enemies, accused him of "having indeed drawn his music from God, but, on the other hand, of doing honor to the devil by indulging in nocturnal festivities with the nuns, who danced to his playing." Luther indeed loved his lute. Matthesius, his friend and companion in 1540, relates, "During the meal and after, the doctor sometimes sang and played the lute. I sang with him."

What form did these house concerts take? We can easily visualize them. Six or eight men are seated around the dining-room table in his home in Wittenberg. It is a cold autumn evening. A cheerful fire illuminates the faces of the singers, which glow with enthusiasm for the music and the beauty of the verses. Two men share the same book, containing in neat script the music for an ode of Horace or Virgil. The musical arrangement is not polyphonic but harmonic, the notes having equal value. Luther, his two sons, Martin and Paul, a few students, and the great humanist, Melanchthon, professor of Greek at Wittenberg, seated around the square table, study the verses in the musical setting, secured from the Salzburg cathedral organist, Hofheimer. Other compositions follow: Josquin motets, and lovely German songs by Walther, Luther's musical adviser in Torgau. The group ends up by singing student songs, and the doctor in person takes his lute and accompanies the song:

> Elsie, my fair one, why dost thou vex me
> That I so long must wait for thee?
> I for thee and thou for me,
> Nothing e'er could better be.

Outside in the market place resounds the horn of the night watchman. He calls:

> Hark ye folk and be you told,
> The clock has just struck ten.

There is consternation over the lateness of the hour. The students and Melanchthon go home. Luther's sons go to bed. The doctor himself withdraws to his study and devotes an hour to reading St. Augustine before he too, weary from the day's work, sinks into sleep.

The boy Luther had a good alto voice which later changed to tenor. German students speak of a "Luther bass," but that is a legend. Once when mention was made of St. Paul's small voice so relates Matthesius, Bohemian preacher at Wittenberg and companion of Luther, the doctor said, "I too have a low, small voice," whereupon Melanchthon said, "But one that is heard far and wide." Erasmus Alberus, the theologian and poet and zealous partisan of Luther, said that Luther had a fine, clear, and pure voice for both speaking and singing. Luther's own words, quoted above, were: *Ich hab auch eine klein und tumpene stimm. Tumpen* was the original Old German for "soft." Luther presumably had a not-too-powerful but good, audible voice. Othmar Rutz, the founder of voice typology, claimed to have arrived at the same conclusion from a study of Luther's prose rhythm. And to the little fantasy just indulged in, we might add some extracts from historical documents, as for instance the humorous letter of January 18, 1535, to the organist Matthias Weller in Freiburg: "We sing as well as we are able, at table, and after. If we make some bad mistakes, that, to be sure, is our fault, and not that of your compositions. For our ability is limited even if we rehearse the music over and over. Therefore you composers must bear with us if we make mistakes in your songs. For we would rather hit the right notes than miss."

Matthesius reports in his wordy style: "When the doctor had worked until he was weary and exhausted, he would make merry at the table, and sometimes started a bit of chanting. In the presence of the right congenial people we would sing Dido's last words, from Virgil's *Dulces exuviae* ("Sweet Spoils"). And Melanchthon also chimes in . . ."

Luther took part in Gregorian chants, as well as masses, motets, and contrapuntal song arrangements. The style of these compositions he characterized well in one of his "Table Talks," displaying more insight into the character of polyphonic music than many musicological treatises of that time. "How strange and wonderful it is," he says, "that one voice sings a simple unpretentious tune (or tenor, as the musicians call it) while three, four, or five other voices are also sung; these voices play and sway in joyful exuberance around the tune and with ever-varying art and tuneful sound wondrously adorn and beautify it, and in a celestial roundelay meet in friendly caress and lovely embrace; so that anyone, having a little understanding, must be moved and greatly wonder, and come to the conclusion that there is nothing rarer in the whole world than a song adorned by so many voices. He must be a coarse clod and not worthy of hearing such charming music, who does not delight in this, and is not moved by such a marvel. He should rather listen to the donkey braying of the [Gregorian] chorale, or the barking of dogs and pigs, than to such music."

Luther was not the only one to criticize the poor and blundering performances of the chorale by musically untrained monks with wretched voices. Many were the complaints coming from other quarters, and Luther all his life spoke disparagingly of these inferior chorale performances.

It is evident from all this that he devotedly loved music and that he fully realized its never-ending possibilities. In a letter he said to Weller, the Freiberg organist: "When you are sad, say to yourself, 'Come! I will strike up a song to my Lord Jesus Christ on the regal [small portable organ], be it *Te Deum Laudamus* or *Benedictus*, for the Scriptures teach me that He rejoices in glad song and the sound of the strings.' So with renewed spirit reach for the claves [keys] and sing until your sad thoughts are driven away, as did David and Elisha."

His "Table Talks" are full of the praise of the "winsome art of music — one of the fairest and most glorious gifts of God, to which Satan is hostile, since it drives away temptation and evil thoughts. The devil does not care for music." And again: "Music is one of the finest of the arts; the notes enliven the text, and it drives away the spirit of sadness, as you may behold with King Saul."

SOME COMMENTS ON MUSIC

Luther's love of music was deeply rooted in his nature and in the vivid impressions of his childhood. We have spoken of the mountain tunes which he heard and sang in his youth and his playing of the lute and the flute. To this we must add the dance, in which Luther also took delight. This is a point which must not be underestimated. "When maidens and youths indulge in folk dancing with suitable music and gesture, it is an *officium humanitatis* and pleases me greatly." At another time he was embarrassed because his presence kept the young people from their dancing. The doctor himself did not join in the dance, as Melanchthon sometimes did; but in his "Table Talks" he expresses himself very sympathetically about this art — a point of view which again reveals his acceptance of the joys of living. This came undoubtedly from his delight in rhythm. Like St. Augustine, he sees in it the element which gives wings to nature and the spirit; and this joy in rhythm finds purest expression in the dances of children. "How can they (convents and monasteries) exist, when Christ says that the singing and dancing of children in the streets is fairer to Him than all the howling and mumbling in the churches; and that the lassies' wreaths and dolls, the laddies' hobby-horses and red shoes, find more favor with Him than all their caps, tonsures, choir gowns, chasubles, and gems? For all this is but child's play, be it admitted, but, since it is play with God's Word, it is not to be compared with the real child's play, but is rather that of monkeys and just plain tomfoolery."

Music, for Luther, is an expression of faith — a gift by the grace of God. He links music with the grace of God, with the experience of God, and with Christ's act of salvation. He who believes in this salvation by Christ cannot help but be happy, and sing and tell about it, so that others may hear it and come to Him. It is not so much a question of whether he can, but that he must; just as the artist *must* express his feelings in color or tones. It is the principle of artistic freedom, which corresponds to the principle of Christian liberty — a liberty which is in sharp contrast to compulsion, to law. "Forced love offends God" is a popular proverb characterizing the compulsion of the old Church. Luther often expressed the idea that music spontaneously flowing from the inmost soul is the image of evangelical freedom, the freedom of the Christian man. "That *lex ira operatur* ('the law works wrath') is evidenced by the fact that Joerg Planck [organist in Zeitz] plays better when he plays for himself than when he plays for others; for what he does to please others, sounds *ex lege* ('from obedience to the law') and where there is *lex* ('law') there is lack of joy;

where there is *gratia* ('grace') there is joy." Again: "What is law does not succeed; what is gospel succeeds. That God preaches the gospel through music is proved by Josquin, whose compositions flow along happily, easily, spontaneously, gently, and, like the song of the finches, are not forced or strained by rules."

What deep insight Luther had into the essence of music — an insight which springs from his philosophy and his theology and, in the last analysis, from his experience of God! What a gap opens up between medieval music and modern music, and, for that matter, between medieval man and modern man as well! Properly speaking, Luther's musicianship anticipated the development of music by three hundred years, for the principle of absolute creative freedom in music was fully realized only by the great classicists, Haydn, Mozart, and Beethoven. These masters created autonomously, expressing their own personalities, regardless of traditional rules and laws.

Ich singe, wie der Vogel singt, der in den Zweigen wohnet ("I sing as does the bird, which lives in the trees") — this artistic creed of Goethe was also that of Luther. At the same time imaginative and realistic, he made no great distinction between the singing of the finches and that of men. And just as he likened the songs of Josquin to those of the finches, so he saw the praises of God in the singing and humming of the forest, in the roar of the sea, in the murmuring of the brook, as well as in the glorious new music of the Flemish and German masters. He sang: "The best time of the year is May, when all the birds are singing." The song of the birds was a favorite of Luther. Whether he told about his feathered friends when at the fortress of Coburg, or from the Wartburg — the blackbird, the lark, or the sparrow — or at another time of the song of the nightingale, drowned out by the proletarian croaking of the frogs, it was ever the natural, the elemental, the spontaneous, that he found symbolized in the song of the birds. Once his little daughter, Magdalena, was asked to sing a song for her cousin, "The Pope Calls to Emperor and King." But when the little girl refused to sing, Luther said: "Nothing good comes from the works of law without grace. What is done by compulsion comes not from the heart, and is not pleasing."

As has been stated above, Luther compared Josquin's works to the song of the finches, because the composer's music flows gaily, gently, and spontaneously, like the bird's song. "He is a unique master of the notes. They must do as he wills, whereas other masters are forced to do as the notes will." This seemingly insignificant remark bears closer examination. Luther's esthetics of music are here expressed in their entirety and reveal the gap between the German music (still deeply anchored in the Gothic) and European music in general, which represented the spirit of the Renaissance, and of which Josquin was the leading exponent. When Luther compared Josquin's music with that of the birds, and contrasted it with that of other composers — older Netherlanders, like Obrecht, and Arcadelt, and the German composers (of whom he says, "They do as the notes will it") — he was thinking of the freely flowing, imaginative tone language of the great master, whose subjectivity was characteristic of the Renaissance. On the other hand, the contrapuntists of the old school, and the Germans, with their archaic constructive style, represented the collective feeling and thinking of the Gothic. Luther had liberated himself from the medieval experience of God, and had accepted the new free experience of grace. But at the same time he clung to the traditional liturgical forms. He stood, so to speak, between two epochs, his face turned joyously toward a new age, but his feet firmly planted in the old.

And thus in Luther's simultaneous devotion to Josquin and the German composers the dualism of his feeling and thinking is revealed. His devotion to the music of Josquin disclosed the love of freedom, the joy of living, which is the spirit of the Renaissance, while his leaning to the German composers, Finck, Walther, and others, links him to the Gothic philosophy to which the joy of an all-forgiving saving love was still foreign.

"Non Moriar sed Vivam"

In 1530 Luther, under the ban of the emperor, was excluded from participation in the Augsburg Diet, so important for the future of Christianity. His patron, the Prince Elector Johann of Saxony, had left him behind in the fortress of Coburg, believing that Luther would be safe from both the pope and the emperor. And while, at Augsburg, the diet made deals and treaties, threatened, appeased, intrigued, and betrayed, Luther, confined in the Saxon border-fortress, was free to glory in the beauties of nature. He delighted in the "lovely dome of God," where at night, in reverent wonder, he would watch the stars appear, and in the day he was wont to hold communion with his beloved birds. The cuckoo called, the nightingale warbled, and, day and night, the ravens and magpies kept up their ceaseless chatter. And he wondered whether they too were holding a Reichstag. . . . It seemed to Luther that "all the papists, sophists, preachers, and clerics have assembled here from the four corners of the earth, so that I might the better understand their wisdom and their lovely singing." What had they now decided? Probably a mighty campaign against corn and malt, for they were already whetting their bills, and were only too well practiced in stealing and robbing. Luther headed his letters: "From the realm of the birds" or "From the diet of the magpies," and here in the Coburg he may have meditated on the nothingness of all temporal things. Temptations and afflictions, both spiritual and physical, assailed him and brought him to the border of despair. To his spiritual doubts and visitations were added physical ills of all kinds: acute pains in the leg, disturbances in blood circulation, which caused him violent headaches, and fainting spells. He slept hardly at all, and in the daytime was overcome by complete exhaustion. He was ready to die, and yearned for the hour of his death. In his despair he wrote to his friend, the great German composer, Senfl. Ludwig Senfl, a native of Switzerland (born in Zurich about 1492, died in Munich, 1555), was one of the most gifted and versatile composers of his time, a church musician of both austerity and charm. He has been compared with Franz Schubert because in his secular songs he has portrayed all the emotions of the human heart. The simple and the sublime, the tender and the robust — he knew how to express them all. Did Luther, who so ardently admired him, know him personally? He might have met him at Innsbruck on his way to Rome, or possibly on the occasion of his trial in Augsburg. At all events, the two men corresponded regularly. Luther's personality must have greatly impressed Senfl. Court composer of the emperor Maximilian I, and later on *musicus intonator* at the Catholic Bavarian court, he was ultimately suspected of heresy because of his correspondence with Luther. He probably lost his position, for after 1540 nothing more is heard of him. Like so many others, Senfl had probably become a martyr to his convictions. Regarded in this light, the letter that Luther, in distress, wrote to his friend gains heightened significance:

"Grace and peace in Christ. Although my name is so hated that I fear that you, my dear Ludwig, will not receive my letter, or if you do, that it may not be safe for you to read it, yet my love of music has overcome this fear. This, my love of music, with which I see my God to have endowed and enriched you, gives me hope that, after all, my letter may not endanger you. For who, even in Turkey, could blame one who loves this art and who praises the artist? I, for my part, esteem your Bavarian dukes although they are surely not well disposed toward me, and I respect them because they cherish and honor music. There are, without doubt, seeds of precious virtues in the hearts of those who are moved by music; whereas those with whom this is not the case must be called blocks and stones. We know that the devil hates and fears music, but I do not hesitate to say that, after theology, there is no art to be placed beside music. Music and theology alone are capable of giving peace and happiness to troubled souls. This plainly proves that the devil, the source of all unhappiness and worries, flees music as much as he does theology. This is why the prophets practiced music as they did no other art. They did not link their theology to geometry, nor to arithmetic, nor to astronomy — but to music, and through music they preached the truth with songs and psalms. But why do I praise music, in that I presume to depict, or rather, to disfigure, so great a matter on so small a sheet? But my heart is full to overflowing with what has so often refreshed me and freed me from grave burdens. I come to you with a plea that you send me a copy of the antiphon, *In pace in id ipsum* ("I will both lay me down in peace and sleep"), if you have one. This melody has comforted me from my earliest days, and all the more now that the words mean so much to me. I have not seen this song set in parts. I do not want to burden you with the task of setting it, but I am assuming that you already have it. I hope that my end is near. The world has no use for me and despises me, and I am weary of the world and despise it; therefore let the Good Shepherd take my soul. This is why I am beginning to sing this song more frequently. But I should like to have it in four parts. If you do not possess it I will send you the notes of the tune and you can set it after my death. The Lord Jesus be with you in eternity. Amen. Forgive my audacity and wordiness. My humble greetings to your choir."

Senfl did not send the requested song until later. He probably had to compose it first. But he did promptly send Luther a musical setting of the One Hundred and Eighteenth Psalm, "I shall not die, but live and declare the works of the Lord." Both the text and the music seem to have reacted like a miracle on Luther. In large letters he wrote the words, *Non moriar sed vivam*, on the wall of his study in Coburg. Luther, having freed himself of his afflictions and doubts, again became the man and the fighter. Music was the panacea that led him back to life and victory, and mankind to truth.

CHAPTER TWO

LUTHER'S CREATIVENESS

At the time of the second diet at Spires in 1529, deep discouragement prevailed among the followers of Luther. Emperor Charles V, after a long feud with the Holy See, was about to make peace with the pope, and one of the conditions made by the pope was the extermination of heresy in Germany. The Catholic majority of the diet had put an effective brake on the propagation of the Reformation. No religious innovation was to be tolerated in the future, and the Catholic Mass was to be held as before. Since these measures once again opened the way for enforcement of the Catholic doctrine in the Lutheran sections of Germany, the Evangelical minority, in a document of protest, declared that no majority had the right to make resolutions in matters of religion. This document was signed by six princes and fourteen cities of the realm. The signatories of this protest against the authority of the pope were designated as Protestants — a name applied later to all dissenters, including Calvinists, Zwinglians, and others. Evil times were now to befall these protesters, struggling for freedom in matters of religion. A renewed persecution of Christians seemed about to break out. In 1527 the

Bavarian cleric, Leonhard Keyser, who had been a close friend of Luther, was tried and found guilty of heresy. Luther, deeply shocked at the death of his friend and follower, put into print the history of this martyrdom, with a moving preface and epilogue.

Brutal tyranny of the anti-Protestant princes, assassinations, and a serious decline in morals were the order of the day. The words of Jacob Sturm, statesman and founder of the Reformation in Alsace, "Christ is again in the hands of Caiaphas and Pilate," speak for themselves. And Luther became firmly convinced that the time of the Antichrist had come, and that Satan was indefatigably at work inciting the mighty of the earth to battle against the Gospel. He was near desperation. But once again, as so often before, his faith in God saved him from doubts and temptations. Even though Satan used all his arts and wiles to tempt him, he found refuge in his God and in the thought that God's Son had died on the Cross for mankind and for him, Martin Luther, as well. *Non moriar* ("not to die, but to live") was the song that once before had saved him from despair. But now a new song struggled through his soul — one that was to become for thousands the song of faith and trust, the triumphant song of the victory of good over evil: *Ein' feste Burg ist unser Gott* ("A mighty Fortress is our God"). This great hymn was probably wrung from the soul of the simple unassuming man under similar afflictions as those in which Beethoven, the great master, poor and deaf, and utterly despairing, created his immortal *An die Freude* ("Hymn to Joy").

Was Luther in truth the creator of the great melody? And how much of a composer was he? Opinions on this subject have undergone great changes in the course of time.

MUSICAL AUTHORSHIP

In the seventeenth century the authorship of more than a hundred hymns was attributed to Luther. This overestimation of the Reformer in musical matters was refuted in the eighteenth century. And the exacting and skeptical research of the nineteenth century, step by step, denied Luther the authorship of any hymns.

A. J. Rambach in his treatise, *About Luther's Services to Church Music* (Hamburg, 1813), was willing to concede to Luther all the melodies, except those known before him. Koch, in his *History of the Chorale* (1847), credits him with eight hymns; the famous musicologist, Carl von Winterfeld, with three, and later writers with none at all. It is only of recent years that Luther has received full recognition as a composer. Today we are of the opinion, represented by the hymnologist, P. Wackernagel (1847), that "in all cases where to one Luther text there existed but one melody, the authorship of the Reformer is undoubted. Only where two or more tunes made their appearance — particularly in his immediate environment — could there be question of other composers."

The present European method of determining the authorship and the originality of a melody makes strict and exclusive demands. Not even the use of single phrases from other sources is permitted if the genuineness of a musical composition is to be admitted. Such matters are treated more freely in America, where, with a sane lack of prejudice, songs are written, the elements of which have been taken over from elsewhere, or well-known compositions are simply syncopated. In older days this modern European individualism was not known, and a utilitarian philosophy, resembling the conception of Oriental peoples, was in vogue. It was not so much a question whether the melody was original. The main consideration was: Which melody is best suited to the poem; has it the maximum of impressiveness and power to capture the largest number of listeners? Music was considered a functional art and not merely art for art's sake.

In Luther's time it was the custom to change secular into religious songs, or older Catholic texts into Protestant ones, always retaining the original melody. These adaptations were called *contrafacta*. In 1574 the seniors of the Bohemian Brethren wrote to the Prince Elector Frederick III of Saxony, referring to their song book: "Our melodies have been adapted from secular songs, and foreigners have at times objected. But our singers have taken into consideration the fact that the people are more easily persuaded to accept the truth by songs whose melodies are well known to them." It was not a question of who created the melody. The purpose counted.

These aesthetics, based on practical principles, require more elucidation.

In his letter to the composer Senfl, the Reformer represented music and theology as closely connected. Luther contrasts arithmetic, geometry, and astronomy with theology and music, that is, the exact sciences with the "humanities." References to the close relation of music and theology often occur in Luther's writings: "Music is a beautiful and glorious gift of God and second only to theology," or "Music drives away the devil and makes people happy," or "Youth should become accustomed to this art, for it makes fine people."

THE RENAISSANCE

Luther's conception of music was rooted in that of the Middle Ages, which again is based on classical antiquity. Accordingly, music primarily has ethical significance. It can make man better or worse, God-loving or Godless; it can actuate his good or his evil instincts. The ancient Greeks attributed certain ethical qualities to the various modes. Socrates wished — if we may believe Plato's *Republic* — to exclude certain tone combinations from the practice of music, as for instance the mixolydian mode (which corresponds to our scale: b a g f e d c b, on the white keys of the piano), "because it is a mournful mode, and useless, even for decent women." And in accordance with the same point of view: "The Lydian mode (our C major scale) is effeminate and intoxicating, while the Dorian mode (E – E on our white keys) is for serious men, preparing them for a warlike career and for the pursuit of peacetime labor." Oriental peoples as well as the ancient Greeks ascribed religious and ethical significance to their various melodies. This applies particularly to the "melody skeletons" (patterns) that form the basis of their music. The Arabs call these melodic schemes *maquams;* the Hindus call them *ragas;* the Javanese, *patets;* and the Jews, *negginoth.* The performances of the *maquams* of the Arabs and the special *ragas* of the Hindus are confined to a specified time and place. These melodies are under special religious protection. Woe to man if a *summer-raga* resounds in winter, or an *evening-maquam* is heard in the morning. Music has the highest religious and especially ethical significance among the primitive races, and in the entire Orient. The Chinese believe that the welfare of a people depends upon the keynote whose pitch is most carefully guarded and kept the same throughout thousands of years. This age-old significance of music has its response in the soul of man; and we read in the book of the ceremonies of Li-Ki: "Music fills the heart with noble feelings, and at the same time appeases the passions. This power constitutes the beauty of music. The mitigating influence of music brings peace. And the cultivation of music has but one aim: perfection."

The medieval conception of music is based on these classical and Oriental ideas.

The old ideas of the interrelation of music and the cosmos (we have only to think of the doctrine of the harmony of the spheres) grew to magical intensity. They were crystallized into the definite conception of music which embraces the entire universe and is divided into three classes: the *Musica mundana* (ordered movement of the universe according to measure and numbers, i.e., the "harmony of the spheres"), the *Musica humana* (which represents the harmony of soul and body with their elementary powers), and the *Musica instrumentalis* (audible music proceeding from the natural instrument, the human voice, or from musical instruments, which are accorded a lower grade).

The Middle Ages adopted this concept from the Roman Boethius, but under the influence of cosmological magical thought, the Greek idea was transformed into one appealing more to the emotions and intellect of medieval man. This is where the Neo-Platonic philosophy of Plotinus set in. The soul, striving to emerge from a world of sensory phenomena — which is but a fleeting plaything and a deceptive reflection of the Real — reaches out for the primeval, the absolute in beauty. The value of music, therefore, lies not in its sensuous magic power, but in its harmony, as a reflection and a resonance of the spiritual, which causes the soul (*eros*) to soar. In the course of time these ideas were more pronounced. Life, and therefore also music and art, are justified only from a metaphysical point of view. Profane music is repudiated. But herewith the gap was opened which proved to be the burden and the curse of the Middle Ages — the gap between good and evil, between profane and sacred music. Christianity, too, took over these aesthetics of art, and subjected music solely to religious purpose.

The Renaissance, however, brought about a change. The secularization of man restored the profane conception of music; and music was cherished again in its own right, regardless of its religious function. The Minnesingers and Troubadours had already sung their songs in praise of benevolent princes and beautiful women, and the great Flemish composers of the fifteenth century had composed not only motets and masses, but gay music, delicate chansons, instrumental pieces which delighted the hearers and had nothing to do with religion.

Luther was a profoundly devout Christian but he was also a realist who stood with both feet in life. He was still deeply anchored in the Gothic Middle Ages, but had absorbed the ideas of the Renaissance. He was fully conscious of the ethical, purifying function of music in the sense of the Middle Ages, and he allowed himself to come under the spell of beautiful music. He wished music to instruct and delight. Therefore he adapted the older church service and introduced simple congregational hymns in the vernacular. He adapted the finest old melodies and folk songs, and created hymns which have never failed to move the hearts of believers.

The introduction of congregational singing gave each member of the church the opportunity to take active part in the church service, thus expressing the idea of a universal lay-priesthood. And, because from now on each and all could approach God in song and speech, religion became infinitely more personal and intimate.

And so the hymn or the chorale came to be the musical foundation of the church service. Luther ascribed to it greatest pedagogical significance, and decreed that children should in earliest youth be taught the elements of music and, above all, of singing. His words concerning the training of teachers and pastors are a case in point: "A schoolmaster must be able to sing, or I will not look at him; nor should one admit young men to the ministry unless they have practiced and studied music at school." The ethical importance given by Luther to music, one of the liberal arts, is manifested when he calls it "a disciplinarian and moral trainer" which makes man "more gentle and refined, more conscientious and sensible. Even poor fiddlers serve a purpose in making us realize what a delicate and fine art music is, for one can the better recognize white when black is placed beside it."

Luther knew well that only hymns sung by the worshipers in a familiar tongue come from the heart, and that therefore only this kind of song had pedagogical value. To be sure, before Luther's time German hymns had been known, but the great majority of religious songs were in Latin.

It is noteworthy that the first German medieval songs developed from the New Testament cry: *Kyrie eleison* ("Lord, have mercy upon us"). The *Kyrie eleison* was heard in the prayers of the peasants in the fields, on pilgrimages, and in church processions. It was prayed, too, by soldiers going into battle. Therefore it is in the *Kyrie* that we must seek the origin of the German hymn. It soon became customary to adapt German words to the slow, measured melodies of the *Kyrie*, and thus the so-called *Leise* (from *Kyrieleis*) developed — mostly four-versed German strophes, ending in the refrain, *Kyrie eleison.*

Music in Battle

On July 9, 1386, at Sempach, fifteen hundred Swiss peasants were victorious over an army of about 5,000 men commanded by Duke Leopold III of Austria. The Austrian defeat meant the final freedom of Switzerland from Austrian rule. The Austrians attributed their defeat to the impetuosity of their young knights, while the Swiss credited Arnold von Winkelried, who sought and found a sacrificial death, with the outcome of the battle, in which for the first time a small band of peasants had defeated a great army of knights.

We know that before the engagement at Sempach, the Austrians, in deep silence, heard the kneeling Swiss solemnly sing the old St. Gallen death song, written and composed by the monk Notker the Stammerer:

> *Inmitten unserer Lebenszeit*
> *Vom Tod sind wir umfangen;*
> *Wen suchen wir, der uns Hilfe gibt*
> *Von dem wir Huld empfangen,*
> *Denn Dich Herre alleine?*
> *Der Du um unsere Missetat*
> *Rechtlichen zürnen tust.*

In the midst of life, behold
Death has girt us round;
Whom for help then shall we pray,
Where shall grace be found?
In Thee, O Lord, alone!
We rue the evil we have done,
That Thy wrath on us hath drawn.

—Tr. by Catherine Winkworth

Evidently the Austrians had no hymn corresponding to the deeply fervid, God-trusting *Leis*, since the chroniclers in that case would not have made special mention of the impression created by the Swiss song.

The battle of Frankenhausen took place May 15, 1525, during the peasants' revolt. When the poor, badly equipped, and misled peasants saw the princes' strong artillery directed against them, they sang the following hymn, in the earnest conviction that they were battling for right and freedom against oppression and slavery.

Nun bitten wir den Heiligen Geist
Um den rechten Glauben allermeist,
Dass er uns behüte an unserem Ende,
Wenn wir sollen heim fahren aus diesem Elende.
Kyrie eleison.

Now crave we of the Holy Ghost,
What of all things we need the most,
True faith in Christ, when life is ending,
And from this grief we home be wending.
Kyrie eleison.

—Tr. by Richard Massie

Luther restored and revived German song, and we may well say that the songs of Schubert, Brahms, Schumann, and Hugo Wolf would have been impossible without Luther. Hans Sachs, the well-known Nuremberg Meistersinger, hailed Luther as the reformer, not only of the Church, but also of German song. In his "Wittenberg Nightingale" he sent Luther the following poetic greeting:

> *Wacht auf, es naht gen den Tag,*
> *Ich höre singen im grünen Hag*
> *Ein wonnigliche Nachtigall;*
> *Ihr Stimm' durchklinget Berg und Tal.*
> *Die Nacht neigt sich gen Occident,*
> *Der Tag geht auf vom Orient,*
> *Die rotbrünstige Morgenröt*
> *Her durch die trüben Wolken geht.*

> Awake, now comes again the day,
> In verdant hedge I hear a lay
> Sung by a wondrous nightingale;
> Its voice resounds through hill and dale.
> The night declines toward the Occident,
> The day comes up from the Orient,
> The dawn in flaming morning rose
> Now through the murky dark cloud goes.

Luther somehow felt that he was inaugurating a new period of song. Characteristic is the opening line of the first song for which he wrote both the words and the music, the song of the two martyrs who died in Brussels for their evangelical faith:

Ein neues Lied wir heben an,
Das walt' Gott unser Herre,
Zu singen, was Gott hat getan
Zu seinem Lob und Ehre.

By help of God I fain would tell
A new and wondrous story,
And sing a marvel that befell
To His great praise and glory.

                              —Tr. by Richard Massie

CONGREGATIONAL SINGING

Luther's greatest concern was to provide hymns for congregational singing. In the *Formula missae et communionis* (1523) he says: "I wish we had more hymns which the people could sing during mass or to accompany the Gradual, the Sanctus, and the Agnus Dei. But the poets are few, or not yet known to us, who could fashion pious and spiritual songs (as St. Paul calls them) that would be fitting to be sung in church. Meanwhile the following may be sung after Communion: *Gott sei gelobet und gebenedeit* ('Praised be the Lord'). We could also use *Nun bitten wir den Heiligen Geist* ('Now crave we of the Holy Ghost'), as well as *Ein Kindlein so löblich* ('An Infant we worship'). For few poets savour of the Spirit. I speak thus to encourage any among you who might be induced to create spiritual songs for us."

Soon after, in 1524, Luther attempted to put his ideas for congregational singing into practice. "We have planned," he wrote to George Spalatin, theologian, chaplain, and secretary to Frederick the Wise of Saxony (who later was Luther's patron and protector), "to follow the example of the prophets and the church fathers and to compose German songs for the German people so that God's Word may resound in the singing of the people. We are seeking poets and musicians everywhere for this purpose. Since the gift has been given you to use the German language in all its fullness, a quality that has been developed by constant practice, I request you to work with us in this matter and try to translate and adapt some of the psalms for singing. Enclosed you will find a copy of my *Aus tiefer Not schrei ich zu Dir* ('Out of the depths I cry to Thee'). I would ask you, however, to avoid new words and the expressions of the court, so that the people may easily understand. Let the words be as simple as possible but at the same time pure and suitable; and see that the meaning be clear and as close as possible to that of the psalms. We must therefore use our own judgment, determine the original meaning, and translate it freely."

Luther did not wait for the help of other poets and musicians. Stirring events inspired him. His first song was the above-mentioned hymn:

> *Zu Brüssel in dem Niederland*
> *Wol durch zween junge Knaben*
> *Hat er sein Wunder macht bekannt*
> *Die er mit seinen Gaben*
> *So reichlich hat gezieret.*

> At Brussels in the Netherlands,
> He hath His banner lifted
> To show His wonders by the hands
> Of two youths, highly gifted
> With rich and heavenly graces.
>
> —Tr. by Richard Massie

In the summer of 1523 two young members of the Augustinian order in Antwerp were burned at the stake in Brussels — the first martyrs of the Reformation. Their names were Heinrich Voes and Johann Esch. As followers of Luther they were sentenced by Nicolaus Egmondanus and Jacob Hoghstraten, the judges of the Inquisition, to die by fire, and even in the flames they proudly affirmed their faith.

The melody of the song is in secular style. Since Luther desired widest circulation, he chose a melody in ballad form. Like all his songs and those of the Meistersingers, this song has two *stollen*, melodically alike, and an *abgesang* — the *stollen* being the opening part, and the *abgesang* the closing part of the song. The rhythm is isometric, i.e., all the notes have the same value, so that the congregation should have no difficulty with it. Luther's melodies are most impressive, whether they express the meaning of the words or suggest the emotions of the author. *Ein neues Lied wir heben an* begins, as does *Ein' feste Burg ist unser Gott*, on three equal repeated notes, like an irrevocable confession of faith. Then the voice falls menacingly, even reproachfully, only to mount again to the flourish *Wohl durch zween junge Knaben* and to rise jubilantly like the trilling of a bird.

The song appeared first in a "one-page print," a year later in Erfurt in the *Enchiridion* (1524), and in Walther's *Hymn Book*.

This brings us to the hymnbooks which were published in Luther's lifetime.

In the preface of the 1524 songbook Justus Jonas, Luther's faithful friend and collaborator, lashes out with brutal frankness against the old ritual, still observed in the cloisters and cathedrals "where — in the manner of the priests of Baal — the chorale is roared, not sung"; and he compares these priests with donkeys braying to a deaf God.

In the same year came the so-called *Acht Lieder Buch* (a book of eight songs). It was of South German origin and was printed in Nürnberg by Jobst Gutknecht. The following year (1525) five more books were published, including *Das Strassburger Enchiridion, Das Nürnberger Enchiridion, Das Strassburger Deutsche Kirchenamt, Das Breslauer Gesangbuch*, and *Das Zwickauer Gesangbuch*. In 1526 appeared, presumably in Magdeburg, the first Low German hymnbook. Others were, in 1529, the *Klug'sche Gesangbuch;* in 1531, the *Gutknechtsche Gesangbuch;* in 1539, the *Hymn Book* of Valent. Schumann in Leipzig; and in 1545, Val Babst's *Hymn Book*, also in Leipzig. Thus we have an abundance of Protestant hymnals, whereas only two Catholic German collections were published, one in 1537 by Michael Vehe and one in 1567 by the deacon of Bautzen, J. Leisentritt.

Ancient Modes

Before discussing the individual hymns of Luther, let us cast a glance at the world of music of that age so different in many respects from ours. The music of the Middle Ages was polyphonic-melodic; today we think in terms of harmony and chords. The musician of the Middle Ages heard two or more voices as individual voices and had but a vague conception of a vertical harmonic interrelation of the tones which he heard. There was a great number of modes. We have but two, major and minor, which have developed from the medieval modes in the course of the centuries. But the basis of medieval music, and consequently of Luther's hymns as well, is the church modes with their Greek names. These they received from the old Greek modes, although they are not identical with them. The discrepancy goes back to medieval theorists, who misinterpreted Greek musical teaching; e.g., the Dorian mode, which in antiquity was based on the scale e f g a b c d e, was converted in the Middle ages to d e f g a b c d. The mode of a medieval melody can generally be recognized by the last note. Hence the old rule which Luther has made proverbial: *Cujus tonus, videtur in fine* (the key or mode of a melody is obvious by its final note). Luther meant this to be taken not only literally but figuratively. The end of a matter will tell its worth.

If we take the "C system," that is, the white keys of the piano, as a basis, then in Luther's time the following finals were possible:

On C — Ionian final
On D — Dorian final
On E — Phrygian final
On F — Lydian final
On G — Mixolydian final
On A — Aeolian final

The last two finals correspond more or less to our major and minor modes. We speak also of Dorian, Phrygian, etc., melodies. If the theme moves in the octave above the basic or final note, we call it an authentic mode. If, however, the melody veers more to the depth, around and under the main tone, we speak of a plagal mode and we add, following the Greeks, the prefix "hypo." Furthermore, these octave scales may be transposed into the "F system" when "B natural" is changed into "B flat."

Luther had a fine understanding of the characteristics of the old modes, a gift which we moderns have lost almost entirely, due to our thinking in harmonies and chords. He sensed the different characteristics of all the modes, e.g., of the hypodorian key he said that it was a *peccator infirmus* ("a vacillating sinner") because at one time it called for "B" and at another time for "B flat." In one of his "Table Talks" he finds fault with the fact that the Passion, *Der Arme Judas*, *Rex Christe*, and the

NAME	"C SYSTEM"			"F SYSTEM"		
	Compass	Final	Con-final	Compass	Final	Con-final
1) Dorian	d – d	d	a	g – g	g	d
2) Hypodorian	a – a	d	a	d – d	g	d
3) Phrygian	e – e	d	b	a – a	a	e
4) Hypophrygian	b – b	e	b	e – e	a	e
5) Lydian	f – f	f	c	b♭ – b♭	b♭	f
6) Hypolydian	c – c	f	c	f – f	b♭	f
7) Mixolydian	g – g	g	d	c – c	c	g
8) Hypomixolydian	d – d	g	d	g – g	c	g
9) Aeolian	a – a	a	e	d – d	d	a
10) Hypoaeolian	e – e	a	e	a – a	d	a
11) Ionian	c – c	c	g	f – f	f	c
12) Hypoionian	g – g	c	g	c – c	f	c

Kyrie eleison were written "in the all-too-gay mixolydian key" (g – g). This and other gay modes were better suited to the *Marienlieder*, as well as "the young lads merrily to the wenches sing." Such a song in a gay key (Ionian in F – our F major) is that of the *"Holy Christian* Church": *Sie ist mir lieb, die reine Magd* ("Dear to me is the pure maiden"). It really begins like a love song, and the Church is glorified in sweet, simple words:

> *Sie ist die Braut,*
> *Dem Herrn vertraut,*
> *Ihr ist weh und muss gebären,*
> *Ein schönes Kind, den edlen Sohn*
> *Und aller Welt ein Herren,*
> *Dem ist sie untertan.*

She stands the Bride
Of Him who died.
Sore travail is upon her.
She bringeth forth a noble Son,
Whom all the world doth honor;
She bows before His throne.

—Tr. by Richard Massie

One can better imagine this song sung to the lute than to the organ. What delicacy, what tenderness in the coloratura, resembling that of the Minnelieder. And some of the phrases sound like a breathless whisper of love. In truth, from *Frauenminne* ("courtship") to divine worship seems but a step.

LUTHER'S HYMNS

One of the most famous songs of Luther is *Nun freut euch liebe Christen gmein* ("Dear Christians, one and all rejoice"). In jubilant strains it calls on the Christian congregation to rejoice and sing because of the miracle of God's redeeming love. This hymn depicts the great facts of our salvation, but in the form of a personal confession. Here Luther's own experience has found strongest and tersest expression. We see the monk in his cell, in anguish and despair struggling for the salvation of his soul; we hear the agonized cry of his conscience: "What shall I do to deserve God's mercy? All is vanity. . . ." But in the meantime:

Meine gute Werke die gelten nicht,
Es war mir in verdorben.
Der frei Will hasset Gotts Gericht,
Er war zum gut erstorben.

My good works could avail me nought,
For they with sin were stained;
Free will against God's judgment sought
And dead to good remained.

Despondency and despair drive him to the depths of hell
and the darkness of death. Then the light of the Gospel
shines for him and he is saved by the mercy of God:

Da jammert' Gott ewigkeit
Mein Elend übermassen,
Er dacht an sein Barmherzigkeit,
Er wollt mir helfen lassen.

Then God beheld my wretched state
With deep commiseration;
He thought upon His mercy great
And willed my soul's salvation.

We now hear the voice of the Father who is sending
His Son. We see the Son, who — to save this lost human
being, to save Martin Luther — has come down to earth,
takes upon Himself the Cross, dies for him, rises, and
returns to His Father. We hear His comforting voice:

Denn ich bin dein,
Und du bist mein,
Und wo ich bleib da sollst du sein,
Uns soll der Feind nicht scheiden.

> For I am thine
> And thou art mine,
> Henceforth my place is also thine;
> The foe shall never part us.

There are no fewer than four melodies to this text, and Luther may have used the folk song, *So weiss ich eins, das mich erfreut das plümlein auff preyter heide* — at least for some of the first publications. His own melody with its energetic fourth (Ionian mode) breathes trust and hope. It became so popular that it was adapted even by the synagogue.

The hymn, *Aus tiefer Not schrei ich zu Dir* ("Out of the depths I cry to Thee"), with its humbly pleading melody, with its sudden drop of a fifth (in the Phrygian mode and deeply serious), depicts the mood of this wondrous paraphrase of Psalm 130. How simple and touching is the passage: *Denn so Du das willst sehen an* ("For if Thou rememberest"). Of special beauty is Simeon's song of praise: *Mit Fried und Freud ich fahr dahin* ("In peace and joy I now depart"). Humility, peace, consolation, and grace emanate from this Dorian melody with its grand flourishes. Its subtle rhythm is better suited for solo singing than for the congregation.

And now the famous Christmas hymn, *Vom Himmel hoch da komm' ich her* ("Good news from heaven the angels bring"). Its text is a paraphrase of the old riddle song, *Ich kam von fremden Landen her*, but Luther created an entirely new melody, to the present day one of the most widely sung Christmas carols. He called it, *Ein Kinderlied auf die Weihnacht vom Kindlein Jesu* ("A Child's Christmas Song of the Infant Jesus"). At first it was sung to the original melody, but Luther was embarrassed to hear the tune of his Christmas hymn sung in inns and dance halls. So he composed the new air in the Ionian mode, that is, in our C major, which in its simple beauty could not fail to touch a child's heart.

What a contrast between this form and the antiphon to the dead, *Mitten wir im Leben sind* ("In the midst of life") in the Phrygian mode! This song goes back to the tenth century and is a free translation of the poem by the St. Gallen monk, Notker the Stammerer, *Media vita in morte sumus*. It was the hymn sung by the Swiss on the eve of the battle of Sempach. According to legend, the monk wrote the poem after seeing, during the construction of a bridge over a ravine, the deadly danger of the workmen suspended over the abyss. This poem became known all over Europe. It was sung in cloisters and in churches in times of plague; by warriors before going into battle; by seamen in distress. In the course of time, people began to use it as a charm so much so that in 1316 the Synod at Cologne ordained that no one might sing it "against anyone without permission." This is probably why Luther undertook a rearrangement of the song, for he was very much opposed to anything heathen or superstitious. In so doing, he made use of the old musical version of Notker.

Heyliger Herre Gott, Heyliger starker Gott,
Du ewiger Gott, lass uns nicht versinken
In des bitteren Todes Not.

Holy Lord and God!
Strong and holy God!
Merciful and holy Saviour!
Eternal God!
Sink us not beneath
Bitter pains of endless death.

—Tr. by Catherine Winkworth

This is a cry for help, strong, compelling — nay, violent. What matter whether Luther wrote the whole melody or only part of it?

"Ein' Feste Burg"

In a document by a Jesuit we read: "Luther has murdered more souls with his songs than with his writings and sermons." Well, of all the "soul-murdering songs," the most murderous, from the Jesuit point of view — the mightiest — is the hymn of hymns, *Ein' feste Burg,* Luther's immortal battle song. In the seventeenth century the poet Philip von Zesen recognized that the rhythm of the hymn resembled the drum roll calls of that century. This is the *Dochmius,* the meter found in the classical drama and predominantly in impassioned lyric sections of Greek tragedy. The many monosyllabic words lend an element of singular solemnity to the poem — something irresistible, joyous and bold, a cry to battle and victory is built up. In the second half of the stanza the hand-to-hand fighting is depicted, guns and lances are outstretched and to the sound of the rhythmic four-time roll of the drums, with short and firm steps, the attack on "the old evil foe" is begun. This song of Luther's, which has led countless Protestant warriors into combat for their faith, has become the battle cry of the faithful against the Antichrist, the hymn of the forces of light against the menacing power of darkness.

Just as the old Latin hymns and antiphons were based on the Psalms, so also are Luther's German chorales. In some songs he followed the biblical text closely, as in *Aus tiefer Not* ("Out of the depths"). In other songs he allows himself more freedom. This is the case with *Ein' feste Burg*, where Luther had in mind the Forty-sixth Psalm which he so incomparably paraphrased. Luther's hymn applied the words of this psalm to the distress of his time, when he feared that, owing to the diet of Spires in 1529, the rule of the Antichrist was nearer than the kingdom of God and that the propagation of the true Word of God had been halted.

There have been attempts, particularly by opponents of the Reformation, to deny Luther's authorship of the melody. That is only natural. The composers of many great melodies have been accused of plagiarism. Haydn was said by the Yugoslav philologist, Kuhac, to have taken his famous "Imperial Anthem" from a Serbian folk song; Rouget de Lisle, the author of the "Marseillaise," was branded a musical thief; and the entire British nation has been charged with stealing "God Save the King" from the French. It is, of course, not difficult to find similarities in the melodies of a single age among a single people and in a single cultural group.

Now let us examine "A Mighty Fortress." The triple repetition of the key tone "C" in the Ionian mode (corresponding to our modern C major scale) is found in many a folk song of German and French origin of that age, and particularly in the organ canzones. (They are the predecessors of Bach's toccatas.) Luther's genius forcefully seizes that triple repetition. The three repeated notes sound like the trumpet blast of a watchman on the tower; they ring out like the fanfares of the Last Judgment which the righteous need not fear; and they give the Christian an unwavering support. They are an outburst of gigantic emotion, of elementary defiance. The joyous, militant, even violent, nature of Luther's faith is nowhere so well expressed as in these first three notes which, in a similar form, if in a different sense, had resounded in the Brussels martyr song. Like a sword, the fourth whizzes over the word *Burg* ("fortress"), only to sink with emphatic and thrice-repeated affirmation to the lower fourth — this time in calm and firm diatonic measures. On the word *unser* ("our"), however, the melody swells in a rising melism as if to say: "It is our God, yours and mine, who was given us in grace" — a joyous, deeply moving experience of God. The next line shows a new picture, *Der alt' böse Feind* ("the old bitter foe"). The line wavers, gradually modulating into the dominant, symbolizing the writhings of the creeping Beelzebub. He coils and rears, then stretches

himself to his full height until he has reached the summit — the *Burg*. The next line marks the struggle of the
two forces. The melody continues to writhe and rear
for the full length of an octave, then falls to the low
"C," the symbol of the inevitable victory of Christian
man. Again the melody halts at the melism, *sein gleichen*
("his equal"). Does it signify the doubt, the seriousness,
of the opposition of the Antichrist? As a matter of fact,
this line would more fittingly express the final verse of
the song, *Das Reich muss uns doch bleiben* ("The kingdom ours remaineth"). And that brings us to the question whether Luther, when he melodized his song,
thought of the last stanza only, and made it the basis
of the rest of the melody. The question whether the
composer of a song has in mind merely the first stanza
or whether he takes into consideration the others as
well has often been discussed, especially by the musicologist, Alfred Heuss. The answer in all probability is
that the composer has been inspired by that stanza which
seems to him the most impressive. The psychological
process is not so simple. The first stanza furnishes the
melodic and rhythmic pattern; but the more a composer
lets the poem in its entirety react on him, the firmer and
more uniform will the melody finally become. Actually
the first bars are not only eminently suited to *Ein' feste
Burg ist unser Gott* ("A mighty Fortress is our God"),
but also to *Und wenn die Welt voll Teufel wär'*
("Though devils all the world should fill"), or to *Das
Wort sie sollen lassen stan* ("The Word they still shall

let remain"). On the other hand, the last musical phrase is so obviously related to the last verse that, when we hear it, the verse occurs to us at once, *Das Reich muss uns doch bleiben* ("The kingdom ours remaineth").

It would seem idle and senseless to dissect Luther's Battle Song and to trace its several motives to Gregorian tunes, as the Catholic hymnologist Wilhelm Bäumker has done. What a fundamental lack of understanding of this brilliant song, so perfectly conceived and molded!

If so disposed, we might find reminiscences in the popular songs of the day, or, predominantly, in the *Meistergesang* ("Mastersinger melody"). The *Feste Burg* perhaps is more closely related to Hans Sachs than to the *Missa de angelis*, which, according to Bäumker, was Luther's model. (Incidentally, this mass belongs to a period after Luther.) Hans Sachs' *Silberweis*, a Protestant paraphrasing of the *Salve Regina*, actually has a strong resemblance to Luther's song, just as the *Meistergesang* breathes a strong Protestant spirit. Here is the *Silberweis*:

ADAPTATIONS AND ARRANGEMENTS

A special chapter should be devoted to the history of Luther's *Ein' feste Burg* after this time. Rarely has a

song been so often adapted. In a collection by Georg
Rhaw (1544) appear no fewer than four contrapuntal
arrangements of the song. Among them are a four-part
arrangement by Rhaw himself (with the melody in the
bass) and a five-part one by Stephan Mahu (with the
melody in the middle voices). These two compositions
Winterfeld has published in his beautiful *Festschrift*
("Memorial Edition") of 1840, but he did not include
the arrangements by Martin Agricola and Lupus Hellinck. Then, in 1586, Lucas Osiander, and in 1597,
Johannes Eccard, shifted the melody to the treble (soprano). Toward the end of the sixteenth century the
trend was to transfer the melody from the tenor to the
soprano. Seventeenth-century arrangements of Luther's
chorale are numerous. In 1730, Johann Sebastian Bach
wrote his magnificent "Reformation Cantata," *Ein' feste
Burg*, in commemoration of the two hundredth anniversary of the day on which the Augsburg Confession was
officially presented. Less well known is Beethoven's
canon, *Ein' feste Burg*, written on January 12, 1825. The
introduction of the Lutheran chorale in Meyerbeer's
opera, "The Huguenots," is better known.

This sensational appropriation caused the indignation
of many Protestants who saw in it a sort of blasphemy.
So thought Robert Schumann in 1837, after the Parisian
premiere of the opera of Meyerbeer. "I am no moralist,"
Schumann declared, "but it outrages a good Protestant
to hear his dearest hymn screamed out on the stage."
Schumann himself toyed with the idea of writing a

Luther oratorio. This oratorio would have had to be quite popular in style to be easily understood by burghers as well as peasants, he said. "I would strive to keep my music quite simple, not in any way artificial, complicated, or contrapuntal, but impressive, pre-eminently effective by means of its melody and rhythm. The oratorio should be suitable for both church and concert hall. Greatest possible fidelity should be observed, particularly in the rendition of Luther's pithy sayings. His relation to music in general, his love for it expressed in hundreds of lovely citations, should not be left out, and the chorale, *Ein' feste Burg*, should come, not before the end but as a great climax."

Among the numerous Luther oratorios mention should be made of *Luther in Worms* by Ludwig Meinardus (1827-96). The work originated in the 1870's, and, of course, the *Feste Burg* forms the close. Luther at first strikes up the hymn alone, and, as more and more voices join in, the spreading of his teachings and the founding of the Lutheran Church are symbolized.

In 1883, Heinrich Zöllner's *Luther Oratorio* was presented in Dorpat, Reval, and St. Petersburg for the four hundredth anniversary of Luther's birth.

Every music lover is acquainted with Mendelssohn's *Reformation Symphony*, which again centers around Luther's chorale. The chorale and certain militant tunes which bear the character of medieval folk songs, as well as the "Luther Amen" (the "Amen," also called the "Dresden Amen," which Wagner has taken over in his

Parsifal) are the musical symbols of this symphony, which is in itself a magnificent confession of the master to his Lutheran faith. Mendelssohn had a follower in Otto Nicolai, who in 1843 composed a church festival overture with a choir, *Ein' feste Burg*, which Franz Liszt in 1852 adapted for the organ.

There are countless organ works based on Luther's theme. Among them should be mentioned the "Organ Variations" of Heinrich Karl Breitenstein, the "Concert Fantasy" of Frederick Lutz, the "Organ Fantasy" of H. Schellenberg, a "Prelude and Fugue" of Karl Stein, another for organ and wind instruments by Karl August Fischer (1828-92), whose older namesake, Michael Gottlieb Fischer (1773-1829) likewise wrote an organ fantasy on the same theme. Müller-Hartung wrote a sonata, Ludwig Riedel a festival overture, to *Ein' feste Burg*. Richard Wagner used the Luther chorale in 1871 for his *Kaisermarsch* (written to celebrate the return of the troops from France). Joachim Raff also wrote an overture, *Ein' feste Burg*, for a drama of the Thirty Years' War, dedicated to Hans von Bülow. Reinecke composed an overture, *Zur Reformations Feier*, and August Bungert a symphonic poem, *Auf der Wartburg*, with utilization of the chorale, which, oddly enough, Heinrich Zöllner had at the same period used for his opera, *Bei Sedan* (Leipzig, 1895). And under no circumstances should Max Reger's "Chorale Fantasy" for organ on the same theme be forgotten.

LUTHER'S MUSICIANSHIP

After this brief excursion into modern times we now return to Luther. One may ask the question: Was Luther a real musician, that is, a professional, or was he just a gifted amateur? The musicologist Hermann Kretzschmar calls Luther the most notable of all amateurs, and classes him with St. Ambrose and Ant. Fr. Thibaut, whose aesthetic treatise, *Von der Reinheit der Tonkunst* ("Of the Purity of Musical Art"), had great influence on the music of the nineteenth century. We could cite other great laymen in music, as, for instance, the shoemaker Hans Sachs, who is of special importance in this connection, because he was a contemporary and adherent of Luther. Can and should we discriminate so strictly between the artist and the amateur? This contrast seems a dubious one, since many a jurist has regarded his hobby as more important than his profession and accomplished great things as a musician. The most important musicologists of the nineteenth century stemmed from juristic circles and from the time of Johann Kuhnau to Handel and Schumann there are instances where the college gown was exchanged for the baton.

In earlier days the distinction between the layman and the professional played no great part; nor was there at that time so great a gap between popular and artistic music as there is today. Music was an affair of the people and it can be assumed that some of the loveliest songs were composed not by professional musicians but by amateurs.

In olden times it was taken for granted that the inventor of a song composed the melody as well as the verse, and once again we refer to Hans Sachs. What the Nürnberger shoemaker was able to do was surely not impossible for Luther.

And speaking of the Mastersingers, let us examine the testimony of the theologian and musician, Cyriacus Spangenberg, who was Luther's house companion from 1542 to 1546. Cyriacus' opinion in the *Cithara Lutheri* (song sermons which appeared in Erfurt in 1569) is significant because he was one of the best connoisseurs of mastersinging. "Luther," he says, "is by far the best and most artistic of all the Mastersingers. Everything flows from him and he is full of charming, delightful fancies. There is spirit and meaning; there is nothing forced, nothing patched, nothing spoiled. His meaning is clear and intelligible. Tune and verse are praiseworthy and heartfelt, and the voice everything that is sweet and pleasing. It all has strength and marrow, so that it heartens and consoles, and forsooth there is no one his equal, much less his master."

In the Middle Ages, during the time of the Minnesingers and the Troubadours, and well into the sixteenth century, the custom prevailed that whoever invented a singable verse and a new meter also fashioned the melody. It was, however, quite another matter when the melody was adapted from another composer and contrapuntally arranged. For the most part, the poets sent their *tenores* (tunes) — either invented by themselves or taken from another melody — to a musician who molded the *tenor* into a contrapuntal form. There are sufficient examples of this practice. A letter written by the composer Sixt Dietrich (1518) to the humanist Bonifaz Amerbach, contains an apology for having changed the music of the little song "since it did not easily lend itself to quadration" (that means, adaptation into four parts).

Of the famous condottiere, Georg von Frundsberg, who met Luther at the diet of Worms in 1521, and who spoke warm words of encouragement to him, his biographer and secretary, Adam Reissner, relates that after the battle of Pavia in 1525, he composed the song *Hofgunst* ("courtly favor"), and often had it sung at table, in four parts, or had it played by instruments when making merry with officers and other guests. The imperial general and chief condottiere himself composed both song and melody, but had another musician (the otherwise little known Caspar Wintzerer) arrange and adapt the song, which version was the one sung by the music-loving condottiere and his companions.

Luther himself in most cases assigned the melodies he invented to other composers for contrapuntalization. But we have evidence that at times he was able to write a polyphonic composition. Among these there is Psalm 118:17, *Non moriar sed vivam et narrabo opera Domini* ("I shall not die, but live, and declare the works of the Lord"). It is the same text for which Senfl sent him the music to Coburg. As we already know, Luther had written the text and tune on the wall of his study, and his physician,

Ratzeberger, saw it as late as 1550. Luther was so strongly impressed by the motet that he decided to write a new composition to the words. A fortunate coincidence has preserved it for us. Joachim Gräff, a poet of the sixteenth century, in his school drama "Lazarus" copied Luther's motet and wrote: "I had this little piece printed because it is so short and not too well known, and used it for my drama." Then follows "*Non moriar sed vivam*, D. M. L."

The little book appeared in Wittenberg in 1554, and there is not the slightest doubt that Luther is the composer of the music just referred to. This piece was formerly believed to have been identical with that of Senfl. However, since Theodor Kroyer in the Zwickau Library has discovered the real motet, all doubts as to Luther's authorship have been dispelled.

Ratzeberger further tells us that at one of Luther's musical parties, *Didonis novissima verba* ("The last words of Dido") by Virgil was sung as set to music by Luther. This composition has evidently been lost.

Moser believes definitely that he has discovered a composition by Luther, since it has the signature of the Reformer in large letters. It is a one-page print with the title, *Klage und bitte zu Gott wider die alten (der alten schlangen) Religion und ihren Schutzherrn* [Psalm 64] (Complaint and prayer to God against the old, i.e., the old serpent's, religion and its prince). The voices (soprano, bass, alto, tenor) are internotated and put into the score to give the simple psalmody.

It is interesting to note that, under the soprano, two

lines of the text are given, and that the bass is notated directly under the soprano. This was done, on the one hand, for the convenience of the figured-bass player, on the other hand, to signify that the two outer voices, bass and soprano, were absolutely necessary. The middle voice could be partly or wholly dispensed with, as happened when the work as a whole was presented monodically, that is, when one singer sang in solo, accompanied only by the organ or the lute. This arrangement was used mostly at hour services (Vespers and Matins).

Luther was well versed in counterpoint. Ratzeberger tells that Luther, singing with his friends, was always ready to detect mispoints and other errors in the music. When he did so, "at once" he took it away and saw to it "that the piece was properly set and rectified."

A Musical Joke

Let us once again tarry with Luther in Coburg, where he was confined during the Augsburg Diet and from where, seriously ill and yearning for death, he wrote the touching letter of which we have already spoken. But even in his most trying periods his sense of humor never entirely left him, and there is another letter of Luther's that is anything but melancholic. It seems to breathe of the spirit of the *Landsknechte* or condottieri, or, rather, the exuberant spirit of the students at Wittenberg. He wrote to Johann Agricola, compatriot, friend, and later opponent, who became unpopular with the Lutherans because of his lukewarmness and because he had assented to the Augsburg "Interim." He had for four days, Luther wrote, been unable either to write or to read, because of headache. Then he found in the *cloaca* a bit of paper on which was written a three-part song. After he had properly improved it and added a fourth voice to it, he requested his Augsburg friends to publish it as a composition of the Augsburg school cantor, and as a song of greeting to Emperor Charles V and Ferdinand I, and as such to return it to him. He would send it to the deacon Rörer in Wittenberg (a puffed-up connoisseur of music who recognized the works of celebrities only) and play a trick on him. What can we gather from the letter? Either Luther composed a fourth voice for the other three (a so-called Vox Vagans) or, what is more probable, he composed the whole piece himself, and as a joke mentioned the unusual place of discovery. He wished to indicate that the piece was good enough for the *cloaca* only. At the same time, however, he desired to prove that his composition was no worse than that of many a celebrity, and that throws an interesting light on the part played by the laity in the musical circles of that day. Luther undoubtedly was a musical genius of high rank, who would have become a great composer, had not Providence destined him to become the prophet of a new age.

The Power of Music

Have some of Luther's compositions been lost? In view of the scant consideration given to music in theological circles, it is quite possible that musical drafts by the Reformer were put aside as unimportant, and then disappeared. Tradition has it that Handel was in possession of Luther manuscripts. Were they in reality compositions, or only melodies like the *Feste Burg*? Was it the German Mass of Luther? Happy the musicologist who — some day — will find these lost treasures.

Indeed, Luther may not have thought his work worth keeping and may simply have discarded his compositions after they had served their purpose, that is, after they had been sung at the churches or schools. But his was a highly creative nature. For him not only creating music, but performing it, had a religious significance. He believed music the best means of encountering temptations of body and mind.

At the close of this chapter we once again quote Luther's biographer, Ratzeberger: "It often happened when Luther was at work in his study that Satan perturbed him in many ways. At one time Lucas Edenberger, preceptor of Duke Ernst of Saxony, came with some musicians to visit him. He learned that Luther had been shut up in his study for some time and had not even requested food. When the door was not opened after repeated knocking, Edenberger looked through the keyhole and saw Luther lying on the floor, unconscious, with arms outstretched. He opened the door by force, raised Luther, and together with his companions began to sing. Dr. Luther gradually regained consciousness, his melancholy and sadness left him, and before long he began to sing with them. He regained his good spirits and

begged Lucas and his companions to visit him often. No
matter what he might be doing they should not allow
themselves to be turned away; for he believed that his
visitations and sadness left him as soon as he heard music."
This, of course, does not pertain to his musical creativeness, but we can assume that, if the power of music alone
could drive away Satan, he envisioned it as a direct communion with God. And so he sings his lovely song, his
praise of music:

Frau Musica

Für aller Freuden auf Erden
Kann niemand kein feiner werden
Denn die ich geb mit meim Singen
Und mit manchem süssen Klingen.
Hie kann nicht sein ein böser Mut,
Wo da singen Gesellen gut.

Hie bleibt kein Zorn, Zank, Hass noch Neid,
Weichen muss alles Herzeleid:
Geiz, Sorg und was sonst hart anleit,
Fährt hin mit aller Traurigkeit.

Auch ist ein jeder des wohl frei,
Dass solche Freud kein Sünde sei,
Sondern auch Gott viel bass gefällt
Denn alle Freud der ganzen Welt.
Dem Teufel sie sein Werk zerstört,
Und verhindert viel böser Mörd.

Das zeugt David, des Kön'ges Tat,
Der dem Saul oft gewehret hat
Mit gutem süssen Harfenspiel,
Dass er in grossen Mord nicht fiel.

Zum Göttlichen Wort und Wahrheit
Macht sie das Herz still und bereit;
Solches hat Eliseus bekannt,
Da er den Geist durchs Harfen fand.

Die beste Zeit im Jahr ist mein,
Da singen alle Vögelein;
Himmel und Erden ist der voll.
Viel gut Gesang da lautet wohl;
Voran die liebe Nachtigall
Macht alles fröhlich überall
Mit ihrem lieblichen Gesang;
Des muss sie haben immer Dank.

Viel mehr der liebe Herre Gott,
Der sie also geschaffen hat,
Zu seiner rechten Sängerin,
Der Musicen eine Meisterin.
Dem singt und springt sie Tag und Nacht,
Seins Lobes sie nichts müde macht;
Den ehrt und lobt auch mein Gesang,
Und sagt ihm einen ewigen Dank.

Dame Music

Of all the joys upon this earth
None has for me a greater worth
Than this I have from my singing,
To set my voice sweetly ringing.
There cannot be an evil mood
Where good fellows sing,
There is no envy, hate nor ire,
Gone is through her all sorrow dire;
Greed, care, and lonely heaviness:
No more do they the heart oppress.

Each man can in his mirth be free
Since such a joy no sin can be,
But God in her more pleasure finds
Than all the joys of earthly minds.
Through her bright power the devil shirks
His sinful, murderous, evil works.

Of this King David's deeds do tell,
Who pacified King Saul so well,
By sweetly playing on the lyre,
And thus escaped his murderous ire.
For truth divine and God's own rede,
The heart of humble faith she'll lead;
Such did Elysius once propound
When his harping the spirit found.

The year's best time is May
With warbling birds on ev'ry tree.
Heaven and earth their voices fill
With right good song and tuneful trill.
And queen of all, the nightingale,
Men's hearts will merrily regale
With music so charmingly gay;
For which be thanks to her for aye.

But thanks be first to God, our Lord,
Who created her by his Word,
For his own beloved songstress,
And for men of music, a mistress.
For our dear Lord she sings her song,
In praise of Him the whole day long;
To Him I give my melody
And thanks in all eternity.

CHAPTER THREE

MUSIC IN THE CHURCH SERVICE

The simplified modern Lutheran church service contrasts sharply with the rich and often elaborate liturgical forms of the early days of Lutheranism. Here, as in many other respects, Luther clung to the old church, and even today we note a strong resemblance between the two rituals.

Until well into the seventeenth century complete masses were celebrated in the Lutheran churches. In the Lutheran ritual, the melodic framework, the *cantus firmus*, on which all parts of the mass are based, is a German chorale.

The impressions of Luther's youth left indelible traces on every phase of his life and work. His musical experiences in Eisenach and in the Erfurt monastery were never forgotten, and during his lifetime he remained devoted to the Latin language and to classical culture. Under no circumstances would he permit the Latin language to be neglected in the school system or in the liturgy. It would be a mistake to think that he unquestioningly accepted everything German, and disregarded the international. We have only to read how he repudiated Agricola's musical teachings (which were arranged in jingle verses), not because they were in German, but simply because Luther felt that Latin was the language for musical instruction. He was of the opinion that every student should learn Latin.

Luther postulated two kinds of divine service. One, a great festive celebration lasting several hours, was designed for churches and cathedrals. In contrast to this, he instituted a simple purely German service for the city and village churches, where the schoolmaster as well as the children knew only German. This short German service, however, was to become the standard for future liturgical development. Broadly speaking, Luther retained the order of the mass. What he rejected were those parts of the mass that ran counter to his theology of the Lord's Supper. The canon of the mass was completely recast.

Luther was of the opinion that the traditional order of the mass, while not essential to the faith, could do no harm. It is valuable for the weak, but must not become an end in itself, as was the case in the old church. As Luther sees it, it is a symbol, a historical and therefore human institution. It has value only as it becomes the expression of a living faith. Luther's doctrine of justification takes from the mass the character of an act in itself pleasing to God, and allows it to exist only as a celebration in which a penitent congregation, through no merit of its own, receives divine grace. As a consequence of this treatment of the mass, a breach was made in the rigidly orthodox edifice of the old liturgy. The wide freedom given soon led to laxness and finally to the dissolution of the mass.

In his *Formula Missae et Communionis* of 1523, Luther ordained a Latin celebration for the chapters and cathedrals, that is, for the richly endowed churches. In considering Luther's Mass, with its strict adherence to the old form, we must distinguish between the sections with permanent text (Kyrie, Gloria, Creed, Sanctus with Hosanna, and Benedictus) and the parts with changing text (Introit, Gradual with Hallelujah, Offertory, and Communion). The latter take into account the particular day in the church year or the feast of the saint in question. Services in honor of the saints, however, were not the general rule among the Protestants, and only a few feasts in honor of the Virgin were retained. The texts of the various songs follow closely the Epistle and Gospel lessons for the individual Sunday. The Introit is the introduction to the mass, mostly in the form of a psalm verse, followed by the Gloria Patri. As a rule, the choir renders this Latin phrase in polyphonic motet form while the minister steps to the altar and, with silent confession of sin, prepares himself for the holy ceremony. Now follow the three-times-repeated Kyrie Eleison and the grand Gloria in Excelsis, sung by the choir in polyphonic motet form. This is followed by the Salutation, "The Lord be with you," the Collects, and the reading of the Epistle. Then follows the Gradual, so called because it was originally sung on the steps (Latin, *gradus*) of the altar, as on a stage, or by the singers standing before the choir loft in the old Christian basilica. The Gradual consists of one or more psalm verses and is sung in the form of a choral composition. Now follows the Hallelujah with its verse, whereupon the Hallelujah is repeated. In the Catholic Church and in the early Lutheran Church, the chanted sequence (a non-biblical text in poetical form) follows here. This the Protestant Church has not continued, with the exception of the Christmas canticle, *Grates nunc omnes*. Occasionally sequences are sung in the Protestant Church on Good Friday, Pentecost, or other holy days. But the Sentence (measured singing carried out without interruption by responses or antiphons), which during Lent takes the place of the Hallelujah, was more or less retained in the evangelical church.

The Gradual soon was omitted from the Lutheran services, and there remained only the "Hallelujah" with its verses, or the Sentence; or the entire part was replaced by a German hymn. Now comes the Salutation, the announcement of the Gospel, and its reading. This reading is not a plain prosaic reading, but is chanted. Next is the Latin creed, chanted in the Lutheran Church by the minister alone, or sometimes with the choir.

This, the first part of the mass, is followed by the German sermon. To be sure, the Roman Catholic Church had known sermons but had assigned to them a subordinate role, whereas in the Lutheran Church they became predominant. This again was a breach in the formal structure of the sacred ceremony. In content, the sermon is based on the Gospel and represents its practical application. After the sermon, the communion liturgy proper begins. Bread and wine are placed on the altar. The Roman Church continues with the Offertory, a psalm verse which can be sung by the choir or by the minister. This section and the so-called *Canon Missae* prayers were dropped by the Lutheran Church. There remained only the Preface, a short introductory prayer. The Sanctus and Hosanna with the Benedictus follow, sung or chanted by the choir. The elevation of the bread and wine had been the center of a bitter quarrel, since Luther recognized the transfigured presence of Christ in the Holy Communion, while Zwingli saw only a commemorative service of the death of Christ and a communion of confession in this ceremony. Calvin, on the other hand, taught that the believer, at the moment of taking Holy Communion, had mysteriously received new spiritual life from the body and blood of Christ.

After the elevation come more prayers and then the *Pax Domini*, the announcement of peace and forgiveness. The culmination of the ceremony is the distribution of the elements, while the choir sings the Agnus Dei. After the Communion, a song is chanted by the choir. The Post-Communion consists of prayers, salutation, and blessing. If no communicants are present, the whole section after the sermon is greatly abbreviated, thus losing more or less all liturgical character.

It is evident that Luther's arrangement of the mass is similar to that of the Roman Church. In liturgics Luther was ever conservative. He tried, in part at least, to conserve the Latin language. He had no objection to the vestments of the Roman Church, nor to the candles, nor to the making of the sign of the cross, nor to the elevation of wine and bread. Little room was given, in this Latin mass of Luther's time, to the congregational hymn, which, following the wish of the Reformer, was to be sung after the Gradual, the Sanctus, and the Agnus Dei. But at the time there were few German hymns; they had first to be created.

The German Mass

It was the idea of a universal priesthood, the idea that the believer himself, without priestly intercession, could and should approach his God, that impelled Luther to depart from the old Latin Mass as the basis of the service when he arranged the German Mass of 1526. He may have been actuated by political considerations, to be sure, for he wished to counteract the radicalism of those enthusiasts who advocated a too drastic eradication of the old ritual. But it must not be imagined that the Latin Mass suddenly disappeared from the Lutheran churches. It continued to be a highly solemn form of divine service. After 1536 complete Latin and German masses, as well as those of a mixed character, were held in Wittenberg.

We must here state that the German Mass is in no

wise a discovery or an invention of Luther alone. Early in 1522, a German mass had been introduced by Kaspar Kantz, the reformer at Nördlingen, but Kantz's mass was nothing more than a mechanical translation of the Roman Mass into German. Important also was the creation of a completely German service by Thomas Münzer, and the more so since thereby he gained great influence over the people. Münzer, the famous Zwickau reformer, who had propagated a religious communism in Germany, had found followers even among Luther's closest friends and adherents. Luther's fellow-professor in Wittenberg, Carlstadt, was so much influenced by Münzer that during Luther's stay at the Wartburg he attempted to reform the church by violence. At Christmas time of the year 1521 Carlstadt held the first German mass in Wittenberg. Thomas Münzer was a radical of radicals who appeared in Thuringia in 1523, made himself pastor of Alstädt, and introduced a German church service there. He was as intolerant as the Roman inquisition, a prophet with apocalyptic visions, a hysterical revolutionary, to whom Luther's teachings were a dead-letter religion. He established committees of enthusiastic "saints" and would have the world ruled by the Holy Ghost himself. With an uncanny power of suggestion he worked on the feelings of the masses. To Luther his speeches seemed like those of a drunkard, but the world listened and greedily drank in his words about the equal distribution of property, the brotherhood of man, a better life for the poor and lowly, and a revolt against unjust rulers. The kingdom of God on earth was to be erected on the ruins of the old social order, and the masses avidly awaited the fulfillment of these promises. Luther endeavored to counteract these tendencies. He left the Wartburg and came to Wittenberg, in spite of the danger that threatened from the imperial ban put upon him. Not everything that Münzer advocated was repudiated by Luther. He knew that a great part of the success of these religious revolutionaries was due to the introduction of the German church services. Münzer had German hymns sung, and some of these have found their way into Lutheran hymnbooks, as, for instance, *Der Heiligen Leben tut stets nach Gott Streben*. The Christmas sequence, *Grates nunc omnes*, paraphrased by Münzer into *Lasst uns alle danksagen*, was also adopted by the Lutherans for their hymnbooks, as was also the "Gloria" melody of Münzer's Easter mass in the form of the song, *Allein Gott in der Höhe*. Münzer's mass was of great significance for the history of Lutheran church music. Luther accepted much of it, adopting what was worth while and positive. Thus he proceeded to perfect the German mass which he conducted for the first time on the Twentieth Sunday after Trinity, October 29, 1525, at the Wittenberg *Schlosskirche*.

In a pamphlet directed against the Enthusiasts in 1524, he wrote: "I would gladly have a German mass today, and I am going to work on it, but I should like it to be of a genuinely German nature, for, although I will tolerate a translation of the Latin text and Latin notes and tunes, I do not approve of it, for it sounds neither right nor pleasant. Both text and music (accent, melody, and gesture) must come from the mother tongue and voice. Otherwise it is but an imitation like that of monkeys."

Here again we must emphasize Luther's unusual sense of the artistic which prevented him from doing things by halves. He was well aware of the fact that if the mass was to be sung in German, the music also would have to be changed. For this purpose, he had the *Kapellmeister*, Konrad Rupsch of Torgau, and the young basso, Johann Walther (who had already published Luther's *Wittenberg Hymnbook*) come to Wittenberg as musical advisers. Of this visit we have an account by the great German composer and musical theorist Michael Praetorius, whose father was a pupil of the first Lutheran cantor, Walther. Praetorius has included the musical memoirs of Walther (written about 1566) in his work, *Syntagma Musicum* (1615-18). Luther's great and sound understanding of music in all its phases is evident from this report:

"When he, Luther, forty years ago desired to introduce the German mass in Wittenberg, he communicated this wish to the Prince Elector of Saxony and to the late Duke Johann. He urged His Electoral Highness to bring the old singing master, the worthy Konrad Rupsch, and me to Wittenberg. At that time he discussed with us the Gregorian chants and the nature of the eight modes, and finally he himself applied the eighth mode to the Epistle and the sixth mode to the Gospel, saying: 'Christ is a kind Lord, and His Words are sweet; therefore we want to take the sixth mode for the Gospel; and because Paul is a serious apostle we want to arrange the eighth mode for the Epistle.' Luther himself wrote the music for the lessons and the words of the institution of the true blood and body of Christ, sang them to me, and wanted to hear my opinion of it. He kept me for three weeks to note down properly the chants of the Gospels and the Epistles, until the first mass was sung in Wittenberg. I had to attend it and to take a copy of this first mass with me to Torgau. And one sees, hears, and understands at once how the Holy Ghost has been active not only in the authors who composed the Latin hymns and set them to music, but in Herr Luther himself, who now has invented most of the poetry and melody of the German chants. And it can be seen from the German Sanctus how he arranged all the notes to the text with the right *accent* and *concent*[1] in masterly fashion. I, at the time, was tempted to ask His Reverence from where he had these pieces and his knowledge; whereupon the dear man laughed at my simplicity. He told me that the poet Virgil had taught him such, he, who is able so artistically to fit his meter and words to the story which he is narrating. All music should be so arranged that its notes are in harmony with the text."

In Luther's German Mass the order of service has remained, on the whole, the same as in the Latin Mass.

---

[1] *Accent* is the actual recitative, *concentus* a more melodious chanting in the Gregorian Chant.

But now everything is presented in German, and to revised chants. After the Epistle, a German hymn is to be sung, for instance, *Nun bitten wir den Heiligen Geist* ("Now we beseech the Holy Ghost"). After this the whole congregation sings the Creed in German, *Wir glauben alle an einen Gott* ("We believe in one God"). The sermon is followed by the announcement of Holy Communion and Luther's Sanctus, *Jesaia dem Propheten das geschah* ("Isaiah the Prophet"), which continues to be sung during the administration of the Lord's Supper. If there are many communicants, other hymns are added. After communion follows the German Agnus Dei, *Christe, du Lamm Gottes* ("O Christ, thou Lamb of God").

MUSIC OF THE MASS

Luther gave greatest attention to the musical arrangement of the German Mass. A glance at his pamphlet on the German Mass confirms Praetorius' statements concerning the modes. As already in the pre-Lutheran Passion music, different tetrachords of the hypolydian mode were used for the *Vox Personarum* (all persons in the story except Christ) and the *Vox Christi*. The repercussion tone — the central tone on which the voice continually dwells, or returns to, after minor deviations — is put a fifth higher for the Evangelist than for the words of Christ. From this evolved the custom, still to be found in the later Passions, of having the Evangelist sing in the tenor voice and Jesus in the bass. This too was of pre-Lutheran origin and goes back to the conception that the higher dignity of Christ is best expressed by a male, i.e., a deep voice.

As for the chanting of the pastor, Luther retained the principle of the Gregorian Chant, but he changed and simplified it. Proof of his linguistic, musical, and psychological insight is the fact that, in using the German language, he dispensed with the melisms and ligatures of the Gregorian chorale, so that only one note fell on each syllable. These principles resemble those advocated by Wagner.

Characteristic is his treatment of the question. Since the question in the German language is generally combined with a rising of the voice, he had the question sung on a somewhat higher note, for instance, *Wer bist du?* or *Ist nicht das Leben mehr wert als die Speise?* A reflection of this can be found in the Passions of the seventeenth century and down to Bach.

In the Roman Mass the Words of Institution of the Holy Communion are not sung but merely murmured. Luther felt obliged to introduce a radical innovation. It may not be out of place to throw more light on this feature of the mass. The words, referring to the significance of Jesus' body and those referring to the blood of the New Testament, are treated musically in a like manner. The German is: *Unser Herr Jesu Christ, in der Nacht da er verraten ward, Nam er das Brod, dankt und brachs, und gabs seynen Jungern und sprach; Nempt hyn und esset, das ist mein leyb, der für euch gegeben wyrd, solches thut so offt yhrs thut, zu meynem gedechtnis.*

("Our Lord Jesus Christ, the night in which he was betrayed, took bread, and when he had given thanks, he brake it, and gave it to his disciples saying: take, eat; this is my body which is given for you. This do in remembrance of me.")

As with other texts which deeply stirred him, this too begins with a high note, "C," stressing the first syllable, *Unser*. Then the voice, as though in humility, drops a third and plays around with "A," then to sink down to the "F" at the second syllable of the word *verraten*, as though expressing deep despair at the misdeeds of His disciple. There, where Jesus himself speaks, *Nempt*, the melody starts in with a low "F" with concise simplicity, moves around this repercussion tone, to rise at the phrase, *für euch*, as if to give melodious expression to salvation by the Saviour's death. What we experience in this simple sequence of tones, full of symbolism, is that deeply personal, sorrowful, yet consoling devotion which radiates from the mystery of the communion as Luther felt it. We meet with it again in the Passions of Bach and in Wagner's *Parsifal*, where this feeling of his is so reverently expressed.

In his German Mass, Luther gives minute instructions for the musical part of the service. At the beginning a spiritual song or psalm is to be sung by the whole choir, and again before the Gospel; during the celebration of the Holy Communion the congregation is to sing the German Sanctus, "God be Praised," the John Huss hymn "Jesus Christ Our Saviour," or the German Agnus Dei.

VARIATIONS IN THE MASS

The mass, in the course of time, was subjected to many changes due to the fact that, after Luther, the pastors and cantors took so much freedom in conducting it. Hence, it was doomed to decay. There was no combination which was not to be found in the Lutheran Mass, not one which had not actually been tried and used. From the end of the sixteenth century on, the mass became more and more abbreviated. In many sections of South Germany, at the end of the sixteenth century, the Latin order of service was entirely omitted, and in others, as in Leipzig, it maintained itself until well into the eighteenth century.

Characteristic of the church service (and this places it in strong contrast to the rigid Catholic observance) is the so-called principle of addition and substitution. The basis, to be sure, was the Latin Mass, but German songs could be added at will to the Latin texts, or these could be replaced by German chants. The elasticity of the Lutheran service finds its origin in Luther's principle of freedom. There were accordingly the following possibilities:

1) the service was entirely Latin;
2) it was entirely German;
3) every Latin prose text could be replaced by a prose translation in German;
4) every Latin or German prose text could be replaced by a German hymn;

5) every Latin or German prose text could have a German hymn added to it;

6) in certain places (before and after the sermon or during the Communion), German hymns could be freely added.

But just as the fixed parts of the old mass — in contrast to the changing sections—were immutable, so in the Protestant Mass the songs of the Ordinary could be replaced only by specified chorales.

The Kyrie by *Gott Vater in Ewigkeit*

The Gloria by *All Ehr und Lob* or *Allein Gott in der Höhe*

The Creed exclusively by *Wir glauben*

The Sanctus exclusively by *Jesaia dem Propheten das geschah*

The Agnus Dei by *O Lamm Gottes unschuldig* or *Christe du Lamm Gottes*.

All other songs but those of the Ordinary had to harmonize with the Church Year. This "de tempore" principle provided an orderly diversity for the Lutheran service, for the basic significance of the day in question was strictly observed. To this the Lutheran liturgy held fast until the days of Johann Sebastian Bach, whose church cantatas are all based on this principle. This accounts not only for the quantity of Bach's church cantatas, but also for their inner richness, their profusion of musical pictures. In his cantatas Bach has interpreted in his inimitable way the meaning of each single Sunday

and holiday. Whether Bach on Christmas Day presents
a great Christmas oratorio, or his cantata, *Dazu ist
erschienen der Sohn Gottes* ("For this there was sent us
Christ the Saviour") or, on the First Sunday of Advent,
Nun komm' der Heiden Heiland ("Come, Thou of man
the Saviour") or, at Trinity, *O Heiliger Geist* ("O Holy
Ghost") or, for the Annunciation, *Wie schön leuchtet
der Morgenstern* ("How bright and fair the morning
star"), he is ever the musical teacher of the congregation.
In consummate style he adapts his text to the meaning
of the day in question, just as the pastor explains the significance of the season of the Church Year.

Hymn Singing

Next to the sermon, the hymn was an important part
of the liturgy. The question comes up as to how and
where it was sung in Luther's time. The hymn was something new in the early Protestant days, new and un-
wanted for the greater part of the congregation. Aside
from the singing of a few hymns tolerated by the church,
the medieval congregation was passive. The ordinary
man was unfamiliar with musical notes. Hymnbooks
were designed for the pastor and cantor alone. Luther
even refused their use to the congregation. The children,
however, learned the hymns and sang them in church.
They became the music teachers of the grown-ups and
boys not infrequently were scattered among the worshipers to carry the latter along during the hymn singing. In addition to the school children, religious and

musical organizations regarded the cultivation of church music as their mission. Noteworthy among them was the "Kaland Brotherhood."

The Kaland Brothers belong to the great group of religious brotherhoods of the Middle Ages. A poem of the thirteenth century ascribes their formation to the sixth century, and names Pope Pelagius II as their founder. Originally the *Kalandae* were clerics of a particular diocese who, on the first of each month (hence the name) met to hold memorial services for their departed brethren. Out of these institutions developed the Kaland Brotherhoods, particularly in Saxony, that is, in Luther's territory. These fraternities consisted mostly of both clerics and laymen, and their mission was the care of and protection for exiles or persons expelled from a community. Here we have apparently the first organizations for the care of refugees. One of the most important functions of these brethren was the holding of public masses, which were sponsored by devout members. In these the brothers personally took part, and it was they who provided the music for the service as well as the pompous burials of their members. Ordinarily a vigil and a mass were read for the soul of the departed. The younger among the brethren, wearing black cloaks and odd-looking hats and carrying burning torches or candles, accompanied the body to its last resting place. Here one of the brothers stepped to the grave and sang a revocation, which was supposed to be the last greeting of the departed from the grave: "Here I lie in dust and ashes, ye, however, prepare yourselves for eternal salvation, whose anteroom is earthly life. . . ."

From the Kaland Brotherhoods, in many parts of Germany, developed the Cantor Schools, organizations that carried out their missions in the field of church music. But in Luther's time there existed Cantor Schools together with the Kaland Brothers and, in addition, the *Kurrende*, of which we have spoken in the first chapter of this book. These organizations were for the most part under the protection of the clerical or secular authorities, or — as in the case of the famous Torgau School (founded by Walther, Luther's friend) — under the protection of a prince. They were the mainstay of Lutheran church music and hymn singing. They acted as a musical cell in the congregation, instructing and guiding those with less musical knowledge. Above all, it was they who sang the contrapuntal arrangements of the hymns, for which higher musical knowledge was a requirement.

Hymn Arrangements

It has been mentioned that the hymns when sung in unison used notes of equal value. This does not mean that the hymns were, in the modern sense, in regular time and rhythm. Just as that age had little feeling for chords and harmony, so it lacked the feeling for metrical music. There were neither bars nor staffs — at least not in vocal music. Instead, only such rhythms were known which progressed from one accented syllable to another. The written form in which the Luther hymns have been handed down to us is either the chorale notation which indicates only the height but not the length of the note, or the mensural notation which can be deciphered only after mastering many complicated rules. The hymns which have come down to us in this manner are, even though transcribed into our modern system of notation, so confusing, with their ever-changing measure, that we can hardly assume that they were originally sung in this form by the congregation. These mensurally notated hymns were sung in unison and isometrically, with notes of equal value. Mensurally notated hymns stem from the polyphonic arrangements performed by trained singers.

What were these polyphonic songs of Luther's time like? The melody with its text was put into the tenor of a four-part arrangement and the other voices played around the tenor melody, entwining it in free polyphony. While the tenor is, of course, vocal, and moves broadly and calmly, the outer voices are instrumentally conceived, and generally played on instruments in lively measures. While the composer does not as a rule invent the *cantus firmus* but takes it from some other source, the other voices are of his own creation. Just as the minister preaches his sermon as an interpretation of the immutable Word of the Lord, so the composer, with his figural voices, interprets the ever static tenor. The tenor symbolizes the eternal Word of God; the additional voices, the exegesis of the believer.

The classic representative of this type of hymn arrangement was Luther's friend and adviser, Johann

Walther. Born in Thuringia in 1496, in the village of Cola (now Kahla), he died in 1570 in Torgau, where he had been a singer in the *Schlosskantorei* and where he was appointed conductor and singingmaster by the Saxon Prince Elector. For financial reasons the chapel was dissolved, and the singers who had been dismissed formed an organization for church music, of which Walther was the head. Through Luther's intervention, the Prince Elector made a grant to the organization. Walther was also employed by the city schools.

It has been mentioned previously that Walther was called by Luther to Wittenberg, to help him plan the music for the German Mass. It was Walther, too, who published the first and most important hymnbook of the Lutheran church: the *Wittenberger Gesangbuch*, 1524, which contained his excellent compositions, contrapuntal arrangements of Protestant hymns, and compositions of other masters.

Walther's hymns, for the most part, are in the above-described style, but there are other compositions written in a more homophonic style. To the *cantus firmus*, carried by the tenor, a simple phrase, mostly without melism or imitation, is added. The simplicity of the theme which makes the text more comprehensible to the listener, since its meaning has not been submerged in the flood of polyphony, was particularly suited to express the idea of Protestantism. Luther desired that the believer approach his God personally, and this could only be accomplished by simplicity of speech and tone.

To be sure, in introducing the new homophonic style Walther could refer to older models. Harmonic and rhythmic simplicity were in the very nature of the Renaissance and humanism, which regarded extravagance of polyphony as an expression of Gothic barbarism.

For centuries at St. Peter's in Rome, the *falso bordone* had been practiced, i.e., the Gregorian Chant was accompanied in parallel thirds and sixths. And the motets of Josquin des Prés and Heinrich Isaak utilized this style cultivated by the Renaissance. Italian popular songs — for instance, the *frottole* derived from them — had long since made use of the harmonic style in their *villanelle, villotte,* and so on. Finally, from the humanistic schools, there emanated a movement with the same end in view. Inspired by the great humanist, Conrad Celtis, musicians of the fifteenth century began to set the odes of Horace to music for four voices, and to scan them metrically, in the style of that time, in long and short syllables. But this required all four voices to declaim the text metrically so that the voices bound together into chords might progress simultaneously. As early as 1450, the famous manuscript collection of the Trent Codices contained such musical adaptations of the antique verse meter. The first printed collection of such ode compositions by Tritonius appeared in 1507 as one of the first musical prints in Germany. It was natural that this form of singing should gain great popularity among the students, since they saw therein an excellent way of becoming acquainted in a practical manner with the meters of the

classics; and it also offered them a good opportunity to
practice a simple melody in several parts. Students have
for centuries continued this form of singing, and in a
work of student music, the so-called *Augsburger Tafel
Konfekt* (1733), this simple contrapuntal form is applied
in a humorous manner. The choruses of the popular
Latin school dramas are written in this simple form. That
Luther, as a student, had practiced this style of music
is evident from his statement, handed down to us by
Praetorius, that he had acquired his musical knowledge
from Virgil. The connection between Latin metrics and
music was deeply implanted in him.

A great number of German musicians had attempted
to compose classical verse in the manner just described:
Cochlaeus, Paul Hofheimer, Benedictus Ducis, Ludwig
Senfl, and others. In the *frottole* by the Venetian publisher, Petrucci, we find such meters in simple themes.
They are just outlines in musical form but without text;
they are designated as "Aer" — the original form for the
word "aria." From these simple unpretentious themes of
the humanists to the four-part chorale of the Protestant
congregation, with melody in the soprano, is but a small
step. The lifeless *falso bordone* style was animated by
the addition of secondary voices; and the rigidity of the
monotonous measured sequence of the voices was miti-
gated by the introduction of variations of great rhythmic
sprightliness. It was the Wittenberg court preacher,
Lucas Osiander, with his *Fifty Sacred Songs and Psalms*,
(1586), who brought this process to a close. He states

in the preface to his collection that the hymns are supposed to be used in the churches and are set "so that the whole Christian congregation can sing them." The fact that Osiander put the melody in the upper voice, in the soprano, after it had been for centuries the special privilege of the tenor, made it possible for the congregation to join in the singing. He writes: "Because of the polyphonic form used until now, a layman who is not proficient in figural music cannot join in the singing, but must listen. For this reason I have wondered how this could be improved, and therefore I have set these fifty songs in such a manner that the whole congregation, even the children, can join in the singing, but have nevertheless retained figural music, which must continue to beautify the song. When the chorale is in the tenor, it is unrecognizable, and the common man does not know what kind of song it is."

Therewith was molded the permanent form of the Protestant chorale, which name emerged at that time. The Königsberg master, Johannes Eccard, in his fifty-five "Songs of the Chorale" (*Lieder auf den Choral*), 1597, the classical work representing this form of the hymn, created this new style of vocal literature. Influenced by the Flemish master, Orlando di Lasso, his collection became a milestone in the history of the Lutheran chorale. Seemingly polyphonic, with the melody in the upper voice, the chorale is accompanied by the other voices, which in continuous rhythmic movement are more or less on their own, without, however, losing their dependence on the leading voice. According to Winterfeld, Eccard is the greatest master of chorale arrangements before Bach.

THE MONODIC PRINCIPLE

We speak of a monodic principle in Protestant church music. This means that the principle described above underlies the Protestant chorale, and with it the church cantata and the religious concerto: the main voice, in the soprano, is accompanied by the other voices depending on it. This method, which seems so natural to us, is by no means so self-evident as would appear. It is the result of a long and complicated development. It is noteworthy that the principle of accompanied monodism, independent of Protestant church music, was developed in Italy about 1600 in opera and solo singing. When humanistically minded music lovers attempted to revive the old Greek tragedy, they experimented with a recitative which became the basis for the aria, accompanied by chords, and also for the homophonic instrumental music of the following age. Monodic Protestant church music is a phenomenon, running parallel with Italian monody, which it preceded, however, by almost two decades. While Italian monody is rooted in the ideas of the Renaissance, Protestant monody is based on the religious independence of Luther and his philosophy and theology. The Italian monody of about 1600 is a relatively late expression of the Renaissance. The time of its rise coincided with the age of the early baroque. The Italian baroque, as embodied in the opera, has from this time on had an element of artificiality. Prima donnas, castrati, virtuosi, and showy coloratura arias and concertos are the expression of this style. Under the influence of Protestantism, however, the development of music in Germany took quite a different turn. Here the upper voice had emancipated itself from the compulsion of polyphony; here, too, is expressed the independence of man who is no longer subject to the rigid law of ecclesiastical authority and hierarchy. Here has arisen a subjective emotional life, based on a new intimate relation of man to God.

Music in Italy expressed the unbridled willfulness of man. It is the image of man himself. The bombastic, boasting pretentiousness of the aria, as well as the concerto, resembles an aristocrat or would-be aristocrat. It chatters and complains in the recitative or the parlando like a haggling commoner, or a jealous prima donna; and in its church music it is solemnly hypocritical. The fervor of Protestant church music, however, lies in the intimate relationship of the believer and God. And yet, Italian baroque and German Protestantism have this in common: the repudiation of authority and the triumph of the individual over the hierarchic collectivism of the Middle Ages.

THE CHORALE

After this generalizing excursion, we resume our discussion of the chorale. The question arises why complicated arrangements of the chorale were at all necessary. Contemporary collections of hymns show us many adaptations of this kind. Today the ill-advised custom of using only one or two stanzas of a hymn, and simply omitting the others is sometimes followed. As an argument against this practice, we must maintain that the Lutheran hymn is something uniform, indivisible, and inviolate. It represents a unified thought; it is a psalm or a part of the catechism or a part of the mass. The consciousness of the uniformity of a hymn like *Ein' feste Burg* was much more pronounced in olden times than in our semireligious age. That is why in early Protestant times all the stanzas were sung. But the hymn was never sung by the congregation alone. It was the custom to alternate between choir and congregation, and the singing was responsive.

This practice goes back to the singing in the ancient Hebrew temple and is justified by the responsory structure of the psalms. In the old Lutheran church the stanzas were divided between the congregation, the choir, and the organ. The congregation always sang "choraliter," that is to say, in unison, and unaccompanied, in equal notes. Never was this singing accompanied by the organ. The choir sang the polyphonic arrangement of the hymn alternating with the congregation; at times the choir and congregation remained silent and the organ played a stanza. In this case the organ was considered a complete substitute for vocal rendition. This is not so easy for the modern churchgoer to understand, but we must realize that the texts were so familiar to the congregation, and the music and words so closely related, that instrumental music could readily be substituted for the singing of the words.

The polyphonic hymn arrangements were by no means sung *a cappella*. From the investigations of Arnold Schering we know that the richly ornamental phrases were sung solely by the voice carrying the *cantus firmus*, while the other voices, more varying and of livelier movement, were generally played by the organ. Other instruments such as strings, lutes, flutes, and cornets took part, particularly on high festivals.

Another musical practice must be noted here, the description of which has been brought down to us by Luther's friend, Wolfgang Musculus, who in his *Itinerarium* (1536) describes the Wittenberg church service of Luther's time. When the choir sang Latin hymns in contrapuntal version, the German versions or similar German hymns were alternately sung by the congregation. For instance, the choir and the organ started with the Christmas sequence, *Grates nunc omnes*, whereupon the congregation in unison sang the second strophe, *Gelobet seist Du Jesu Christ*, and so on.

The church service in the Gothic cathedral, with its altar paintings, sculptures, and stained glass windows — giving only a dim light — presented a colorfully impressive picture. The singing of the minister or the choir boys, alternating with the congregation or the choir, gave the service an uplifting, joyous, and jubilant tone.

The hymn was interspersed with the playing of the organ alone, to give the worshiper time for silent meditation.

MUSICAL INSTRUMENTS

And now the question arises: "What part did the organ play in the Lutheran church service?" Musical instruments played an important part in the life and thinking of Luther. We have already stressed the fact that he was a good lute player. Again and again we find reference to musical instruments in his expositions, Bible exegeses, and sermons. At one time he compared God, who wishes to convert man, to a skilled lute teacher who shows his pupils one thing after the other, beginning with the easy and increasing to the most difficult. The pupil, however, thinks that, once he knows how to twang the strings, he has grasped the art. When he can draw sounds from the lute he boasts that he has mastered everything.

Luther gave an allegorical interpretation of the musical instruments mentioned in the Hundred and Fiftieth Psalm: the instruments mentioned there can be regarded as the various kinds of sermons: the trumpet represents a sermon on theology, the reference there being to the production of sounds without the use of the human hand; the psaltery represents the teaching of good works; the harp speaks of sin and suffering; the drums, of a penitential sermon; the choir, of the unity of the church; the strings, of diverse teachings; the organ, of great and heroic things, such as the life of the martyrs; the cymbals, of spiritual consolation, jubilation, and the certainty of eternal glory. At another time Luther meditates how the trumpet sounds on sad occasions, but the trombone for joyous, festive celebrations — the one weeping with the sad, the other rejoicing with the happy. And again he compares the outward show of sanctimoniousness with the lead pipes of the organ that squawk and whine in church and yet have neither words nor meaning. As a rude peasant does not understand the marvelous relations between the sounds of the organ or harp because he does not comprehend the meaning and spirit of their harmonies, so many of us do not understand the ways of God's providence. Now that we are speaking of Luther's musical similes, let us recall this metaphor:

"In music, the leading tone is the Gospel, the other notes the law, and as the law is softened by the Gospel, so the Gospel dominates the other tones and is the sweetest of voices."

In medieval musical theory the "mi" and "fa" determine the character of the key and have a softening sweet effect in the quality of a leading tone. The rigidity of the law which makes it a sin not to obey is symbolized by the fixed notes (in C major: ut, re, sol, la), while the notes e flat, e, and f, which determine the key, represent the grace of the Gospel.

The Organ

Of all the instruments, the organ is of course the most essential for the church service. From early youth,

Luther appreciated the music of the church organ. He presumably tried his hand at this instrument, for the organ has always played a prominent part in his imagination. In 1542 he wrote: "Sing to the Lord a new song. For a miracle a hymn of thanksgiving and prayer should be sung. And this is the new miracle of God, that He through His beloved Son has divided the true Dead Sea, and redeemed us from the Pharaoh, Satan. It is for us to sing a new song, namely, the Holy Gospel, and to thank God therefor, so help us God. The music of the following psalm should help us to sing such a song. And so should Wolff Heintz, with his organ, symphonies, virginal, regal, and what else there may be of music. And in this new part, a gift of God, of which neither David nor Solomon, nor Persia, Greece, or Rome knew anything, let him proceed singing and playing joyously in praise of the Father of all grace. Amen." It is evident that this remark was meant for the organist, Wolff Heintz, or for someone close to him. The listing of the instruments could refer to the church in Halle which had two organs, symphonies (orchestras), a virginal (harpsichord), regal (portable organ), etc.

Most of Luther's church orders take no notice of the organ. In some of these orders organ playing was not forbidden, provided neither love songs nor otherwise licentious songs were sung to it, and that the playing was not of long duration — so as not to detract attention from the service itself. The custom of allowing the organ to be substituted for congregational hymns could lead to some embarrassment, for the organist might be tempted to give vent to his virtuosity and supplement his playing with too many artistic flourishes. Finally, the use of secular songs by organists might be criticized by all-too-moralizing contemporaries. To be sure, both text and melody of many secular songs were put into use for church music, but most of them were repudiated. These were called *Schamlieder* ("licentious songs"), and deemed improper by both Catholics and Protestants. The organ tablatures of that day show many such songs, German, French, and Italian, and doubtless the organists played their own adaptations of these songs in the churches. These organ tablatures also contain German dances, *pavanes*, *balletti*, etc., that were played in 4/4 time, and continued as *proportz* ("hops") in lively triple measure. The organists who served the regular organ as well as the portable one, in church, at home, or on the dance floors may not have been too discriminating in the use of this music. In the fifteenth century the same pieces were heard everywhere: in church, in the ballroom of a prince or a rich merchant, and at the weddings of the middle class; and later — after the Reformation — the same tunes were used in churches. It is therefore easy to understand why the church authorities kept a watchful eye on the music played on the church organ.

The organist played from the organ tablature. This tablature in Germany, as well as in other countries, consisted entirely of letters, in contrast to the complicated mensural notation used by the choir. Over the letters,

dots and dashes, as well as little flags (*caudae*) indicated
the length of the notes. Bars were first used in the tablatures. Our modern notation has adapted them, along
with the stems of such notes as eighths and sixteenths. As
a rule the organist himself arranged his tablatures from
printed or written collections of vocal composition —
masses, hymns, and motets — adapting his music for the
organ. As was the technical term of that day, he "in-
tablated" the compositions. The two German tablatures,
the older and the younger, differed in that the older
gave the highest voice in a mensural note, while the
younger notated all parts in letters.

From Luther's monastery days comes a charming story
concerning the customs just mentioned. From his sta-
tion at Erfurt he conducted services in the village, and
once — when in full array he was about to approach the
altar and begin the mass — the sexton, out of a clear sky,
played Kyrie, Gloria, and the Pater Noster on his lute.
Luther could hardly keep from laughing: "For I was
not accustomed to such organ playing and had to adjust
my Gloria to his Kyrie. . . ." It is evident from this that
it was customary to play all the parts of the mass instrumentally.

Luther's remark that he could scarcely refrain from
laughing when he heard the sexton begin the strange mass
indicates that the great Reformer disapproved of these
excrescences in church music.

With all his deep appreciation of music Luther well
knew that it was spirituality that was all-important. In

this respect he associated music with devotion to the Lord: "As beautifully as the angels can only he sing who by faith lives an angelic life." "What I call singing," he says at another time, "is not alone droning or shouting, but every sermon or public confession should be in praise of the Lord's work, admonition, grace, help, consolation, victory, and salvation."

Once he deplored the fact that so many people attributed the charm of the psalms to music alone, whereas the psalms should be judged by their spiritual content, even though music did enhance their beauty. Above all, Luther was opposed to the baroque extravagances in music, for he regarded theatrical pomp in music as an expression of work-righteousness. Therefore he said in his first lecture on the psalms: "Psalms and music exist to stimulate the fear of the Lord; when they resound in impure tones, however, they destroy the spirit rather than edify it." At times he actually fulminated against music in the church. "As in the time of King Manasseh the cries of the burning children were drowned out by music and drums, so now church music drowns out the ruin of souls." In the exposition of the Magnificat he bemoans that "now the whole world is full of church service and singing and praise, preaching, organ playing, and piping, and the Magnificat is beautifully sung — but it is lamentable how little the deeper meaning of the hymn is grasped."

From such passages as these it can be perceived how Luther, who was so deeply bound up in music, did not hesitate a moment to abandon his beloved art when it did not fulfill its true purpose: serving God alone.

COMPOSERS AND PUBLISHERS

We should not close this chapter on the direct relations of Luther to music without making clear who were the musicians with whom he came in contact, and which of these he esteemed most highly. Of some we have already spoken, as Josquin des Prés. Mention has also been made of his great friend in music, Johann Walther, and of Edenberger and the organist Joerg Blank, and of Wolff Heintz. The principal publisher of Lutheran church music was Georg Rhaw, a man who lived and worked in Wittenberg under the eyes of Luther. Theologians know Rhaw because in 1519 in Leipzig he wrote a twelve-part mass, *De Sancto Spiritu*, on the occasion of the Reformer's debate with Dr. Eck. Rhaw, a compatriot of Luther, was born in Eisfeld in the Thuringian forest. He studied at the University of Leipzig, and as cantor of the church of St. Thomas in the same city he was a predecessor of Bach. It appears that casting his lot with Luther in the Leipzig debate cost him his position. He had to retire to Wittenberg, where he wrote a musical primer and in 1524 began his activities as a publisher. How close his relationship with Luther was is evident from the preface which Luther wrote for his *Symphoniae jucundae* (1538), in which he declared that music is of divine origin, insolubly bound to the

Holy Scriptures and the best means of spreading the truth, being in itself a divine service.

In the years that followed Rhaw published a number of masses and other musical selections for divine services. In 1544 — four years before his death — he wrote in a preface that he felt his end approaching and he considered himself fortunate to have completed his series of works in church music. The importance of Rhaw's labor lies in that he was the only publisher to edit a complete work of Lutheran church music; and just as important is the fact that he gave predominance to Protestant composers. He became still more popular through his *Neue deutsche Geistliche Lieder für die Gemeindeschulen,* of 1544. These hymns are identical in style with those of Johann Walther. Rhaw's collection is of importance because from it we learn which of the musicians were more favored by Luther. For it was under Luther's eyes and supervision that the works of Rhaw appeared.

In Rhaw's German hymn collection Thomas Stoltzer, a contemporary of Isaak, Finck, and Josquin, is the oldest contributor. The Reformation came when he was an old man and he was probably not too much in sympathy with it. However, in the year 1526, at the wishes of Queen Maria of Hungary, whose court conductor he was, and of Duke Albrecht of Prussia, he set several psalms in Luther's translation to music, one of which is enclosed in Rhaw's collection. Ludwig Senfl, of whom we have already spoken, is also represented. A third prominent master is Arnold von Bruck. He was conductor at the Catholic court of Emperor Ferdinand I. Since he composed the music for Stephan Zirler's song, "Henceforth I will be a good Papist and despise Luther," it has been claimed that he was converted from Protestantism to Catholicism. However, officially he was never a Protestant. That he deeply sympathized with Lutheranism is evident from the fact that he composed music for a whole series of Luther's hymns, for instance, *Komm Heiliger Geist, Gott Vater wohn' uns bei, Mitten wir im Leben sind* (Ott, 1534). From a contemporary source we can gather that they were written for the presentation of the Augsburg Confession.

How deeply this composer felt the distress of his day is evidenced by his song, *O allmächtiger Gott*, a prayer to God to end the strife which was tearing Christendom apart. Of the life of Stephen Mahu, who was conductor for Ferdinand I, we know little. He, as well as Arnold and Senfl (to whom Luther sent his famous letter), was "officially" Catholic, but a "silent" Protestant. Lupus Hellinck held a church position in Bruges (Belgium) at the time when Charles V and Marguerite of Austria tried to suppress the Reformation. He too was a "silent" Protestant. But not all contributors to Rhaw's collections were such "silent" Protestants. The actual representatives of Protestant music were men who were openly and genuinely Lutheran. Benedictus Ducis, whose real name was Herzog, was a pupil of Isaak. When he was converted to Lutheranism, he lost his position as court conductor and had to accept a small pastorate near Ulm. Contemporary documents speak of him as "exiled for the truth," and probably in theology, also, he became a leader. The same can be said of Balthasar Resinarius, whose official title was bishop of Böhmisch-Leipa. He was a Bohemian Hussite and a member of the Bohemian Brotherhood. And just as Luther took over a number of songs from the Bohemian Brothers, so many of Resinarius' compositions were published by Rhaw. The true type of Protestant musician is Sixt Dietrich, the southern counterpart, so to speak, of Johann Walther. Born in Augsburg in 1492, he received his education in the singing school of the cathedral at Constance and at the universities of Freiburg and Strassburg. He was a highly educated humanist and musician and was in contact with the most prominent scholars of the day. A deeply devout Protestant, he saw the heroic struggle of Constance against Charles V, in which the imperial city refused to give up its faith. When the imperial troops had finally taken a suburb of Constance, they carried the sick Dietrich to St. Gall, where he died in the same year (1548). From 1540 on he had visited Wittenberg several times and was in constant touch with Luther. We may assume that he supervised the printing of his own compositions at Rhaw's establishment.

Wolff Heintz was organist at Halle and Magdeburg, and in the Smalcald War he was the leader of the Halle citizenry. That he was one of Luther's intimate circle is evident from the quotation given above and from a letter written him by Luther. Another musician appearing in Rhaw's printed works is Johann Weimann, an organist of Nürnberg, who died in Wittenberg in 1542. He undoubtedly was close to the Reformer.

It was not Rhaw alone who made Wittenberg the center of Protestant church music, but it was above all the strong personality and prophetic gift of Luther which attracted so many fine musicians to Wittenberg. And here again we are concerned with the question: Who are the composers of the anonymous pieces of Rhaw's collection? May not one or another of the songs in this collection be by Luther himself, who modestly wished to remain in the background as a creative musician? The research in this field of early Protestant church music is still in its beginnings. An exhaustive investigation of the material may bring many a surprise.

CHAPTER FOUR

FROM LUTHER TO BACH

Lutheranism had no rigidly organized church behind it as had Catholicism. It was a doctrine of the free and voluntary submission of the human to the divine will, a doctrine resting on the principle of the grace of God, a grace which embraces all humanity, and on belief in the personal priesthood of each believer, requiring no mediation.

It was a doctrine which must appeal to the inner man. But lacking the rigid system of the Catholic Church, Lutheranism could as little withstand this external power as it could hold its own against the more consistent organization of Calvinism.

Influence of Calvinism

Luther's personality did indeed have an authoritative effect during the four decades after the Reformation; but even during his lifetime dissensions arose among his followers. To this was added the growing power of Calvinism. The hostility between the two confessions grew so bitter after the Synod of Dort (1618-19) that many Lutherans believed it wiser to unite with the Catholics against the Calvinists than to join with the Calvinists against the Catholics. This inner rift has had its ill effect up to the present day. The Catholic Counter-Reformation did not fail to profit by it. It had, in the Order of the Jesuits, an advocate of mighty eloquence and conviction, and an assailant of enormous thrusting power. The Jesuit schools flourished. However, a reaction which soon set in was the cause of the founding and growth of Protestant universities and high schools. But the Counter-Reformation attracted art to the rich Catholic courts, where the artists were more generously treated than in the German Protestant cities whose power was steadily decreasing.

Luther's conception of his doctrine had been purely religious; but after his death the social, cultural, and political contrast between Protestant and Catholic came to light. This contrast went parallel with that between the aristocracy and the middle class, between the court and the city, and this disparity manifested itself particularly in the use of language. It had been Luther's wish that the German language might become the general language for the church service, but that liturgical functions and the choral singing might be in Latin. But a sharp reaction on this question set in. Attempts were made to abolish the ritual and discard the foreign language of the Catholic service. Only orthodox Lutherans tolerated the Latin Mass; and more radical still were the Calvinists. Their Puritan conception of worship as a period of instruction, their merely symbolical understanding of the Lord's Supper, and their moral and pedagogic philosophy and theology brought about a growing antagonism to the mass and organ playing. The Lutherans were gradually influenced by these views. Music as an art was only tolerated and, as time went on, it came to be regarded as a papist horror and abomination. Where the mass was still held it was abbreviated and was retained only in the form of the *Missa Brevis*. The hymn alone remained the unquestioned requisite of the Lutheran service, whereas the Calvinists, because of its musical and therefore worldly basis, rejected even that. Consequently they began to create their own hymns on the sole basis of the psalter. Clement Marot's first psalm-poems were enthusiastically received at the French court, above all by Francis I, who induced Marot to present the psalms to Charles V, Catherine de Medici, Marguerite of Navarre, Henry II, and many other celebrities who used them. But the Catholic circles soon realized the danger of the wide popularity of these psalm paraphrases and forbade them; and so the beautiful and deeply moving verses disappeared from the castles of the French aristocrats and the boudoirs of the fine ladies.

After Marot's death, Theodore Beza, a friend of Calvin, continued the writing of psalm-hymns; and soon afterward these psalms were put to music — first by Guillaume le Franc in 1552, and later, in 1561, by Louis Bourgeois. But the greatest of these was Claude Goudimel (born 1505 at Besancon), who composed eight volumes of the Marot-Beza psalters. Goudimel, one of the most prominent musicians of his day, was a Huguenot and was murdered in the St. Bartholomew massacre.

It is interesting to observe in the Goudimel psalters how the requirements of church music went hand in hand with the general musico-historical development. Goudimel's first psalm compositions (1551) are broad in structure and in polyphonic motet form; later he put the psalter into more condensed form, in simpler composition, and in 1565 his psalter appeared in perfectly simple four-voiced movements. It is based on the melodies of le Franc and Bourgeois, and in this form it has come to be the basis of Calvinistic hymnody. The influence of the Goudimel psalter on Lutheran church music was considerable.

Lutheranism and Calvinism

The difference between Calvinism and Lutheranism, viewed from the standpoint of music, is that the former had no possibilities of development because it denied all aesthetic function to music, whereas Lutheranism bore within itself immense artistic possibilities. It is fitting here to clarify the difference between Lutheranism and Calvinism and from this to draw definite conclusions as to its effect on the history of music.

At the center of Calvin's theology is the doctrine of predestination, which may be summed up as follows. God from eternity has destined a certain specified number of human beings as chosen for beatification, regardless of their merit; all the others are damned. Such a conception serves to emphasize the unbounded self-glorification of God. The doctrine of predestination governs the whole life of the Calvinist. The believer strives to lead the life of one of the elect and feels himself but the instrument of God to carry out the divine plan.

The Lutheran, on the other hand, knows of no such election to grace. He believes that all men are redeemed by the death of Christ, and are elected by God for salvation, if they are the followers of the true gospel. In this sense Prof. Otto A. Piper in his essay, "The Political Structure of Lutheranism," makes the following distinction: "According to the Lutheran view the assurance of a person's salvation rests upon his vocation, whereas Calvinism regards his election as the basis. . . . Vocation, in the sense in which Luther and his followers understood the term, is a direct divine interference in a person's life. God enters into the believer's experience in order to save him. God is thought of as *Deus loquens,* i.e., a God whose very nature it is to address himself to the minds of the individuals. Through His Word and the Sacraments, especially through baptism, God indicates to the individual that He loves him, and therefore wants him to live as His child in constant communion with Him. Election, on the other hand, in the sense in which Calvinism understands the term, is an act of the transcendent God and only indirectly by its effects upon the spiritual life of the individual can election be experienced. By the act of vocation, in the Lutheran sense, God calls the individual into the historical church as the congregation of the saints; election in the Calvinistic sense is meant to make him a member of the future kingdom of Christ."

Dilthey defines the difference as follows: "When contrasted with the Calvinistic belief with its somber earnestness, its consciousness of unconditional duty to God — how different is the character of Luther's idea with its wide comprehensive grasp of the whole man, its radiant joy in the natural, and its transfigured activeness."

We have only to read the words concerning the life of the Christian in Calvin's *Institutes:* "It is the duty of the believers to offer to God their bodies as a living sacrifice, acceptable to God. We are dedicated, consecrated to God. So we can hereafter think nothing, speak nothing, act nothing, but in His glory. For whatever is sacred to Him *cannot without great wrong to Him be employed for profane uses.* We do not belong to ourselves, so we must forget ourselves and whatever we possess. We belong to the Lord and every part of our lives, as the one legitimate purpose, must be dedicated to Him."

How different Luther's words when he speaks of the faith of man: "Is not that a happy household, where the rich noble bridegroom Christ takes for His wife the poor despised human soul?" Luther's positive relation to the world, his joy in living, rest on his conviction that the world itself is not bad, but that the evil is within ourselves. We cannot please God by turning away from the world or by asceticism; but only by a joyous faith in salvation through Christ. It would therefore be presumption and rebellion, nay, sin, to reject the gifts of God. The power of Christ in this world is so great that the devil can do no harm. But inasmuch as we must resist and overcome Satan, Luther sets forth that positive, vigorous philosophy of life which produced such characters as Schütz, Handel, and Bach.

The Calvinist conception: The Invisible God and His Word alone fill the mansions of His Church, and even pictures or other images of Christ and crucifixes are not tolerated, because the worldly visible, the human, and with it the aesthetic, have no part in divine worship. Thus music played a very unimportant role in the Calvinistic service.

Added to all this, with characteristic liberty Luther permitted (and it was Luther's personal wish) the inclusion of non-Protestant music for the service. "For," he said, "the devil should not have all the beautiful melodies for himself alone."

Luther had placed full responsibility on man himself for his attitude toward God. Man was thus placed face to face with his God without any priestly intercession; but it was in a congregation only that he could develop his individuality and fulfill his task toward himself as well as toward the community and God. A development in favor of the personal in man now set in. Whereas early Protestantism had placed collective thought in the foreground, it now followed that the believer stood out more as an individual. The Church became a refuge for those suffering from the world and its ills.

And this development is of great importance in a musical sense. The church service continued to be primarily congregational, but the worshiper demanded newer, more intimate forms. These feelings expressed themselves in the newly appearing song arrangements. The early Lutheran composers, like Johann Walther, treated the hymn to be set to music as a symbol of the Word of God. "The Word they still shall let remain" also referred to the *cantus firmus* of the church song. It was immovable and eternal. The other voices were ornamental and exegetical. Those composers attempted to express the Word of God. Not so their followers — they began to interpret the Word, to illustrate it, to bring it into closer relation with their own thoughts and feelings. The spirit of the baroque had also taken possession of the Protestant Church.

The Motet

The musical form corresponding to this spirit was the motet, the multivoiced arrangement of a psalm verse or a Bible verse. Psalms or other Bible words formed the texts. The word "motet" stems from the French *mot* (word). In the thirteenth century a musical piece called motet was a composition where several (usually three) voices sang together in different rhythmical figures. Such a piece had, as a rule, a Gregorian *cantus firmus* as its basis; over it the upper voices counterpointed in individual but different texts, often using worldly airs. And at the same time the voices, rhythmically speaking, were independent of each other. The Netherlanders of the fifteenth century, above all Jean de Okeghem, perfected this style, which was to become the standard for the motet: the polyphony with freer and closer imitation of all the voices. And this was the style that Protestant motets took over.

The Flemish master, Orlando di Lasso (1532-94), had the greatest influence on the development of Protestant music, although he himself was not a Protestant. Born in Belgium, he had traveled to Italy, France, and England and had developed into one of the great cosmopolitan musicians of the time. He received a permanent appointment at the Bavarian court in Munich. Over two thousand works of this versatile musician, who was at home in all styles of compositions and whose inventiveness and creativeness are astonishing to us, have been preserved. We are interested here only in his hymns and psalms, with their novel and very personal interpretation of the texts and their symbolized and tone-pictorial details of composition. His penitential psalms of 1565, which Duke Albrecht of Bavaria had Hans Mielich publish in an edition de luxe, are of an impressive plastic quality that leads directly to Bach. It is a most personal and noble expression of that style of music which was designated by his contemporaries as *musica reservata*. Lasso influenced many Protestant masters. His most prominent pupils were the South Tyrolian, Leonhard Lechner (1550-1606) and the Thuringian, Eccard (1553-1611), the organist for the Fuggers in Augsburg who later was Prussian *kapellmeister* in Königsberg. The *Lieder auf*

den Choral ("songs based on the chorale") are filled with
a calm, firm trust in God. They are in simple counterpoint and show great mastery in the treatment of the
choir setting — quite in contrast to the impassioned,
deeply felt, and sensuously glowing song motets of
Lechner. The latter's work, *Sprüche von Leben und Tod*
("Sayings about life and death") contains, among
others, that masterpiece of a genius, *O Tod Du bist ein
bitter Gallen* ("O death, you are a bitter gall"), which
has been compared to the medieval dances of death. It
is of demonic impressiveness and could not be surpassed
by any modern composer. Other prominent masters in
the field of the motet are Michael Praetorius (1571-1621),
and Hans Leo Hassler (1564-1612). The latter was
kapellmeister of the imperial court at Vienna and Prague
and a musician of great universality (he had studied in
Venice with Andreas Gabrieli). He was a Catholic who
composed Protestant music. Michael Praetorius, on the
other hand, was the typical representative of Lutheranism. He died in Wolfenbüttel as imperial conductor but
was at the same time conductor at Halle and Dresden.
In his chief work, *Musae Sioniae* (in nine parts, 1606-10),
his superiority in motet music is indicated. In his song
motets the chorale is simple and easily grasped, while his
treatment of the other voices (see his *Nun komm', der
Heiden Heiland* ["O come, Saviour of the heathen"])
is characteristic of the individualizing tendencies of the
time.

These composers represented the two generations following Luther. The form which they used was the biblical motet. Whereas the Catholic composers of religious music held strictly to the authoritative liturgical texts, we now see how the Protestants, carrying their principle of freedom into the liturgy, made use of every kind of biblical text for their musical creations. Gospel passages or entire Gospel lessons were used for the various Sundays and holidays, as were arrangements of the psalms.

Medieval man accepted the Word of God as something static, and he would not have dared to make any changes therein. He could assert his individuality by purely technical means, such as polyphony and declamation, but further than that he dared not go. It was the art of Lasso and his pupils only, which worked a change. It cannot be emphasized enough that all these tendencies toward individualism (deeply rooted though they were in Humanism and the Renaissance) had been influenced decisively by Luther's doctrine. In realistic dramatic manner, musicians depict the happenings of the outer world and all the spiritual emotions — resurrection, death, heaven and hell, God and Satan, forgiveness, happiness and despair, repentance and atonement, resignation and revolt, light and dark. All these feelings and emotions that we find recorded in the Bible have found, in the works of these composers, resounding reverberation.

The call to God, the anguish of the passion, the confession of the sinner — all these are the subjects of this *ars reservata*. The use of the double- and multi-voiced technique of contrasting question and answer, by means of a double chorus, was a new musical method. This technique has hitherto been ascribed to the Venetian, Giovanni Gabrieli (1557-1612) alone. He and his uncle Andreas Gabrieli before him, inspired by two organs at St. Mark's in Venice, had written alternating choruses — *chori spezzati.*

But of late it has been pointed out that this style was cultivated not only in Italy, but in Germany too, and is based on Protestant music as well as on Italian. The antiphonal principle is inherent in the Christian rite, which again is based on the Jewish ritual, as we know it from Philo's description of the Therapeuts in Alexandria and other documents of Hellenistic Judaism.

It is important to note that the principle of the double chorus — which in musical as well as in other respects resembles the symmetric formations of baroque architecture — corresponds with the new religious dynamics and with the idea of a new direct relation to God.

INTERNATIONALITY OF MUSIC

The Thirty Years' War brought with it a wave of internationalism from which all of Protestant church music profited. The concert and choral style of Gabrieli, the new monodic form as inaugurated in Florence and Rome, the growing importance of instrumental music, the new means of expression (chromatics and daring harmonies) greatly influenced Protestant music. Lutheranism, following the principle of its master, could adopt these forms and measures, and of course did.

Michael Praetorius, a Protestant of purest mettle, still used the old motetic-polyphonic method of writing, but he also employed the madrigal form, the concerto style of composition. Praetorius belongs to the older school and is, to a certain extent, to be contrasted with the three masters, no less important than he: Johann H. Schein (1586-1630), Samuel Scheidt (1587-1654) and the great Heinrich Schütz (1585-1672). These three composers of the baroque have been called "the three great S's."

Schein was Bach's predecessor as cantor of St. Thomas at Leipzig, where he resided after 1616. In many respects he can be compared with Praetorius, particularly in adopting the Italian concerto style. But while Praetorius entirely disregarded the Italian monody, Schein fell captive to that new form of expressive art. He discarded the old strictly orthodox form; the chorale was changed and made the object of an extraordinarily subjective concerto method. This style is found in his work *Opella Nova* (1618). Here Schein leans to the baroque Italian style of Monteverdi, whose expressionistic art is carried over into the Protestant experience of God. Schein delved deeply into the meaning of the biblical texts and tried to express their spiritual message in music. An endless scale of emotions, of tension and fulfillment, characterizes his music. Arioso and recitative dramatically change off, and all the possibilities of concerto and monodic style are employed. We have but to hear the dialogue between the angel and the Virgin Mary in his "Annunciation," for soprano, tenor, four trumpets, and figured bass: *Maria, gegrüsst seist du holdselige, der Herr ist mit dir* ("Hail, Mary, thou that art highly favored, the Lord is with thee"). The manner in which, under supreme tension, the angel addresses the Virgin, the repetition: *Maria, Maria* (effected here by recitation of a strongly emotional phrase, a second higher), and the deep humility and breathless suspense, in Mary's answer: *Welch ein Gruss* ("What a greeting") prove him to be the great master of the baroque.

INFLUENCE OF MYSTICISM

Luther's religion is fulfilled in the service which man owes to God, in the subjection of his own will to the commandments of the Lord. It had been the anguish of Luther's own soul, even when a monk, that he could not fulfill the unconditional demands made by God. All natural piety seeks self even in its good works: the sense of duty to God is everywhere hurt and broken. "Man finds nothing within himself to make him pious." He feels only the enormous disparity and breaks himself against the Absolute. And he is therefore definitely guilty. But Luther had the courage to face divine judgment. And it is here that the God-experience, the experience we call "grace," begins — beyond which there is nothing.

It is easy to understand that this stern conception of God had to give way in the new and more subjective age with its changed philosophy. The tremendous gap between the ego and God had to make place for a diminishing distance between man and God — for a union of man and God. . . .

Luther himself was greatly imbued with mysticism. His is the Christ-mysticism as it is found in St. John and St. Paul. "Faith unites the soul with Christ, as a bride with the bridegroom." For the mystic the deciding experience is the birth of God in his soul: God and the ego become one. God is born in the depth of man's nature, in the depth of his soul — a depth too far removed to be reached by the mind and the senses. Jacob Boehme says: "There is something in the soul that is so related to God that it is one with God — not only united." This profundity of the soul, where man and God are united, is cluttered up with the debris of life and the world. The mystic aims to remove this and to turn to the inner man. The decline of the senses is the beginning of truth.

In the mystic work, *Theologia Deutsch*, we read: "All being, all creation, all ego, must be lost and sink into nothingness. The soul must be pure and clean and void of all substance. This is the quintessence of mysticism. The consciousness of the ego must be destroyed, for to the conception of oneness, all substance, all individuality, all independence are impossible." Therefore Angelus Silesius can say: "I myself am eternity, when I leave time. I am as rich as God, when I meet myself in God and God in me. There is no atom of dust, believe me, that I have not in common with Him." And elsewhere this mystic says: "I know that God without me cannot live one mite. Have I come to nought, He must in distress give up His soul. I am as great as God, He is as small as I; He cannot be above me, nor can I below Him be."

This flowing and blending of the soul with God, in which God is a friend and a kind Lord, and Christ is the sweet bridegroom, had a deep effect on religious beliefs of the seventeenth century. When man seeks and finds God in his own soul, he can identify his feelings and thoughts with God. The worship of God became an ardently mystic inner experience. Boehme, a shoemaker dedicated to mysticism, wrote in "The Rise of Rose-Colored Morn": "Had I but a divine pen to write about the spirit of revelation! I have learned no more about the great secret than a stammering child that is learning to walk. The tongue of man cannot explain what the spirit conceives and understands."

The era of the Thirty Years' War was devoted to mysticism, not alone among the religious leaders but among laymen as well. Alchemism, astrology, and cabalism flourished. Whatever the secular or the religious mystics wished to express in the unwieldly language of those days was but a searching, a stammering, for expression. And perhaps because language could not give expression to thoughts and feelings, help was sought in the language of tones, and music became the means of expression for the mystic ideas of the day. What poets and scholars could but scantily put into words the musician could supply with adequate voice. By means of the new technical methods he had acquired he could find within himself the ecstatic music which led to a union with God, for in the depth of his soul, imbedded in the *Harmonia Mundana*, rested God, the primal source of all creation, the creative force of the All. Music, God, and the world were one to the musician of that day.

HEINRICH SCHUTZ

The Protestant musician, who had become imbued with the spirit of mysticism, proceeded to put all forms of music into the service of his faith. This was freely done by Schein and Scheidt. Scheidt was both orthodox and a mystic. His chief importance lies in the fact that he greatly influenced his contemporaries by his works, *Cantionae Sacrae* and *Deutsche Konzerte*. Through him the sacred concerto became the dominant form of Lutheran church music. Even the titles of his works give evidence of the hold that mysticism and the baroque had on him, as for instance in his last concert work, *Liebliche Kraftbluemlein aus des Heiligen Geist Lustgarten, abgebrochen und zum Vorgeschmack des Ewigen Lebens in Zwei stimmigen Himmelschor versetzt* (1635).[1] In his sparse use of Italian monody he closely approached the orthodoxy of Praetorius.

The high light of mystic feeling in the seventeenth century is represented in the personality of Heinrich

---

[1] Because of its extravagant German baroque form this title cannot be adequately translated.

Schütz, a great man and musician. "An artist who is the equal of Bach," says Abert, in his *Musiklexikon*. This intellectual giant towers sky high over his contemporaries. Born in Köstritz, Thuringia, he was conductor of the landgrave of Hessen, Moritz, "the Learned," in Kassel. The landgrave had Schütz educated in the aristocratic school, Collegium Mauritianum, where he studied law at the wish of his parents. But he went twice to Italy, "the blessed land of music," where in 1609 he studied under Giovanni Gabrieli until 1612, the year of the latter's death. Intermittently he was active in several German cities, and was a student in Leipzig until the Prince of Saxony called him to his court. There he soon became *kapellmeister* and remained so (with a few interruptions when he spent some time in Brunswick and Copenhagen) for fifty-five years until his death in 1672.

Schütz's great accomplishment was his fusing of the two trends of thought, the traditional-orthodox and the personal-mystic, into a higher unity. He was a devotee of the church service strictly in the sense of Luther, and at the same time experienced all the glow of mystic ecstasy. Schütz is the representative of the feeling and thinking of the Protestant man of his time, wavering between orthodoxy and rationalism on one side, and mysticism and emotionalism on the other, and very often fusing one with the other.

The effect of the dialogues of the "Song of Songs," as for instance the *Kommt zu mir* ("Come to me") is tremendous; as though the composer wished by force to

call for a union with God, the *Unio Mystica*. Imbued
with deep mysticism is the "Geistliche Konzert" (1636):
O süsser, o freundlicher Herr Jesu Christ — o wie ver-
langet meiner Seelen nach Dir — ach dass ich bald zu
Dir kommen könnte ("O sweet, kind Lord Jesus Christ
— O how my soul longs for Thee — ah, could I but come
to Thee soon"). It is profoundly mystical. It is a devotion, a tremulous adoration of Christ, a religiosity aim-
ing to lead to mortification, to a dissolution of self. It
expresses in tones — and therefore more beautifully and
in general more intelligibly — what the mystic in his
inadequate language would say.

> *Soll ich mein letztes End und ersten Anfang finden,*
> *So muss ich mich in Gott und Gott in mir ergründen*
> *Und werden das, was Er. Ich muss ein Schein im Schein,*
> *Ich muss ein Wort im Wort, ein Gott im Gotte sein.*

> To find last end and first beginning
> I must myself in God and God in me discover,
> And be as He. I must be
> A light in light, a word in word,
> A God in God.

Let us take the psalm: "Hear me, O God, when I call
upon Thee." The two voices, beginning in canon form,
are like the clasped hands of angels pleading in almost
voluptuous yearning for God. At the same time the
believer listens deep within himself, and the second voice
seems to him to be the echo or rather the resonance of
his soul, and therefore the mystic God himself. In truth,

the works of Schütz are the expression in music of the thoughts of Silesius and Boehme.

However, his Passions, "St. John" and "St. Matthew," are of an order quite different. Here it is the word that is in the foreground, the stern word of the Bible, which to him, the true Lutheran, is law, immutable and unalterable. This music is simple, profoundly earnest, and almost primitive. It would almost seem as if the artist dared not disclose what was deep in his soul.

PIETISM

The development of Protestantism, from the period of the outgoing sixteenth century to the beginning of the eighteenth, is marked by a sharp contrast between orthodoxy and a pietism arising out of mysticism. At the same time the existence of the church was threatened more and more by the philosophy of the Enlightenment. A diminution in interest in the church, and a loss of its temporal powers, followed.

In Luther's time, music had become an integral part of the church service. The church service was intimately connected with the life and feelings of the people. That, of course, was also true of the church music. The ideas of humanism brought about a breach in this unity. The increasing culture of the higher classes and the infiltration of rationalistic ideas shook the foundations of faith; and so the art of Schütz, with its ecstatic mystical music, became an art of the individual, which appealed more to the intellectual attitude of the aristocrats and the rich burghers than to the people's feelings and thoughts. The hymn, which in Luther's time had been closely associated with the people, now lost its significance, and was superseded by the "spiritual concerto." But once again it was destined to be revived when pietism reformed the clerical and social life of Germany.

A prominent precursor of pietism was the theologian Johann Arndt (1555-1621), who with his *Wahres Christentum* ("True Christianity") had a momentous effect on contemporary Germany. He wanted to impregnate life with the sanctifying power of Christianity. He spoke in tones of calm contemplation and admonition. It was the touch "of the heart pulse of a personality entirely dedicated to God." Arndt's purpose was to lead a Christendom lost in externals back to the things of the inner life; in so doing he turned to Christian mysticism. He typified and taught a Christianity in life in and through God. It was on his ideas that pietism was constructed; and doubtless the musical art of the great mystics (among them Schütz) drew inspiration from Arndt's writings.

It was Philip Jacob Spener (1635-1705) whose famous work *Pia Desideria* ("Pious Wishes") gave enormous impetus to the movement. Spener demanded a more thorough knowledge of the Bible, at home and in the churches, a more profound devotion on the part of the ministry. The Christianity of knowledge should be replaced by a Christianity of action; Christian ideas were to be unceasingly propagated. For this purpose small circles, resembling somewhat our Sunday schools and church clubs, were instituted, and soon pietism developed into a mass movement governing all fields of private and public life.

As, immediately after Luther's death, theologians began to disagree among themselves, so now Spener's doctrine called forth heated discussions. G. K. Dilfeld of Nordhausen (1678) denied the orthodoxy of Spener's faith, which Spener, however, could prove by his doctrine of justification, of original sin, and of the Trinity. There are, to be sure, elements of enlightenment in Spener's teaching, for — strange as it may seem — enlightenment and pietism in many respects went hand in hand. Spener makes godliness largely dependent on the moral will and the responsible decision of the individual himself. These are rationalistic thoughts, which contradict the mystic ideas of the bridal union with Christ and the complete submersion of the individual in God.

Spener was accused of heterodoxy, intolerance, bigotry, and rationalism, and soon violent opposition arose to his teachings. A new, radical, and aggressive pietism now developed, particularly at the university of Halle on the Saale. Its chief leader was A. H. Francke. On the one hand, charitable work was started. Francke instituted an orphanage, furthered foreign missions, and founded a Bible Society. On the other hand, he preached contempt of science, renunciation of all worldly amusements, as well as of secular literature, theater, dance, and all youthful pleasures. The Halle men adopted from mysticism a strange ecstatic bliss, a consuming, almost voluptuous yearning for death, and a reveling in the sanguinary aspect of the crucifixion. Paul Gerhardt's *O Haupt voll Blut und Wunden* ("O Sacred Head, Now Wounded") has presented to thousands the image of the Saviour in anguish. This submerging of self in the agony of Christ leads the mystic to the urge for union with the Saviour, by suffering, himself, the agony of Christ and so becoming united with Him.

Untold feuds between the "Hallensers" and their opponents characterized the epoch, such as the struggle between Francke and the philosopher, Christian Wolff, which led to the expulsion of Wolff from the university by order of King Frederick William I. The unconverted were looked down upon by those "enlightened by grace" and were barred from Holy Communion. Pietism, originally a movement of the masses, had now become a literary affair of the higher classes. Württemberg alone retained its popular character. By 1740 the Halle pietism was on the wane.

MORAVIANISM

We cannot conclude this sketch of the religious movements of the era without alluding to the Herrnhuter community. This brotherhood, which grew out of the increased emigration of the Bohemian Brothers of Saxony and Silesia, chose the Zinzendorf estates in Upper Lusatia as the field for its activities. They called their colony, which was under the leadership of Christian David, *Herrnhut*. This community was a church within the church in the manner of Spener and his pietism. They recognized three groups, according to their membership in the three different churches, i.e., the Lutheran, the Reformed, and the Moravian. Later, however, they regarded themselves solely as adherents to the Augsburg Confession. The Herrnhuter considered the personal communion of the individual with the Saviour and the inner experience of his own salvation the essential feature of their religion, which was quite in contrast to a simple acceptance of any doctrine. Their whole life was based on this assumption. The dogmatic teaching was abolished with the exception of such fundamental truths as the reconciliation of all mankind, and the demand that the believer experience in his own heart the living truth of the redemption through the death of Christ. The leading spirit of the Brotherhood was Nikolaus Ludwig, Count von Zinzendorf. His religious importance lies in the unique form of his devotion, which, in his passionate love of the Saviour, represents a special type of pietism. Zinzendorf replaced the "mystical union" with an almost erotic worship of Christ, predominantly of the dead body and the blood of the Saviour. Another example of this trend is the following: "I long to embrace Thee, bleeding Saviour. Thou art bleeding from a thousand wounds. Oh, could I touch these dripping wounds!"

Zinzendorf's religiosity was suffused with images of Christ's agony. In his "Swiss Speeches" he affirms that he does not need association with human beings, for he is in communion with the Holy Ghost, who constantly depicts for him the Saviour in the image of a martyr. This impassioned physical experience of Christ in all the phases of his earthly pilgrimage and his death — all this signifies the crown of life, the true godliness.

The atmosphere of the true Christian is saturated not only with the images of the Christ Passion — it breathes the very embodiment of Christ. Even the air surrounding the body of Christ has become the object of his imagination. A favorite expression of Zinzendorf was *Kreuzluft Voegelein* ("the bird which flies around the Cross"). The wounds of the Saviour are the object of profoundest veneration. In his "Pennsylvanian Speeches," so called because they were made in Pennsylvania, he makes the wounds of Jesus his subject matter, to prove how these wounds can be felt and kissed. In the "Litany of Wounds" they are the object of an ecstatic adoration. The first chorus sings: "Oh, hallowed Wounds — miracle-working Wounds"; the second chorus answers: "So wet and bleeding they bleed my heart, so I remain with courage and with wounds." This "blood of Jesus" religion actually led to a "theology of blood": No theological or philosophical revelation could bring bliss to the believer but "the blood of Christ" alone.

Music naturally was influenced by these religious trends. But since Zinzendorf, with all his extravagant ideas, held firmly to Luther's faith, and orthodoxy was ever the exponent of Lutheranism, the chorale continued to be the basis of church music.

Pietism, as a continuation of the older mysticism, affected music from within, but, on the other hand, its purism, the negation of all joy in living, was bound, in a sense, to neutralize more artistic music. Spener, and also Francke and Zinzendorf, held that only the simple hymn was permissible, at times with an organ accompaniment. This, of necessity, caused an ascendance of the sacred song. Spener himself was a composer of religious songs, but the most prominent of these song writers was Paul Gerhardt (1607-76). A nondogmatic mystically devout belief emanates from these poems, many of which were put to music by Johann Crüger. Some of them have gained fame the world over through their use by Bach, as *O Haupt voll Blut und Wunden* (after the medieval *Salve caput Cruentatum*) and many others.[2] The greater part of the songs by Zinzendorf, Neander, and Richter were at first sung in the homes, and only later and gradually taken up in the churches. Their music was often cheap, borrowed from French *bergerettes* and operatic arias.

The Church Cantata

Up to this time the old motet (and later the spiritual concert) was the standard musical form. Both conformed to the style of preaching, even when the manner in which the Word was proclaimed was — like the style of Schein and Schütz — personal, subjective, often agitated and mystical. The pietistic philosophy and poetry,

---

[2] Others include *Nun ruhen alle Wälder, Wie soll ich dich empfangen, Befiehl du deine Wege,* and *Ist Gott für mich.*

with its wealth of imaginative depictions, were conducive to contemplation.

Like the secular cantata, the church cantata consists of the dramatic recitative (narrator and persons) and the contemplative aria which were the means of expressing religious feeling and devotion in music. The motet was gradually discarded and became a secondary feature, but the *Kurrende* still sang these in the streets at Christmas and Easter, and for weddings, funerals, and other celebrations.

Thus the cantata came to be a religious service in itself and combined all its parts into one form adequate to the baroque mind. For as the baroque period looks for types in all phases of life and in all forms of art as well (in architecture, in the laying out of gardens, in social ceremonials), so it finds in the opera certain definitely determined psychological situations and conceptions. As the opera composer has typical means of expression at his command, when he writes an aria of vengeance, when he lets the scorned lover die, or when he builds up a finale, so the composer of the cantata also finds typical means of expressing the language of the Evangelists, the contemplative chorale and the message of Christ. It is the typical that the baroque requires and welcomes. And this is the reason why the cantata which was so closely related to the opera soon conquered the Church.

While the church music of the Reformation era placed the written word (as symbolized in the chorale) in the foreground, the early baroque (Schein and Schütz) emphasized the interpretation of the Scriptures. The post-Schütz period (the high baroque Hammerschmidt, Pachelbel, Buxtehude) introduced free contemplative texts. The word of the Scriptures was neglected and its interpretation became the main feature. The result was the *Erbauungs Kantate* ("the Edification Cantata"). The composers Johann Kuhnau, Georg Boehm, and others cultivated this form.

This individual interpretation reached its summit in Johann Sebastian Bach. A superior personality made the cantata form his own and revealed itself with unequaled inspiration. While Bach's precursors had been preachers of the Word, the cantor of St. Thomas became the last great prophet of the Word of God, as Protestantism conceived it.

It must again be emphasized here that this highly personal religion of Bach and its artistic expression in music would have been impossible without the doctrine of the grace of God, and of Christian liberty. Luther had gained the assurance that divine justice is not gained by man's endeavors but is a gift of God himself. Out of this creed, in which man, conscious of his nothingness and unworthiness as a sinner, gratefully accepts the gift of divine forgiveness, there naturally grew — free from law — the joyous surrender of the individual will to that of God.

This experience is filled with joy and beauty, full of

gratitude and jubilation, and bound up with the glories of the earth.

Upon this rests the history of Lutheran church music, with its principle of freedom in the liturgy, which made possible the adoption of all proper forms of music, but which also made it possible for all spiritual tendencies of Protestantism to find a haven in its music.

CHAPTER FIVE

THE PASSION

In a small and little-known treatise, R. Benz, a German writer whose observations are worth examining, writes that the Passion of Bach may be called "The Tragedy of the North." It is more than that: it is "The Mystery of Christian Man."

What is the meaning of the "Mystery"? It seeks to put into words the inexpressible, to make clear the incomprehensible, and to fathom what we can but imagine. And for Christian man the most profound of all secrets is divine grace, granted to him by the death of the Saviour. God through the death of Christ has freed man from his sins and has brought him salvation; and to the believer the death of Christ is the symbol of a truly Christian life.

As Easter draws near and we are about to listen to a Bach Passion, the sacred awe, the solemn expectancy of one approaching a holy mystic shrine may overcome us. The presentation of the agony of Christ, His death and resurrection, must stir the believer to the depth of his soul; man realizes that between his becoming and being, between his life, his world, and his family, and Christ and His earthly pilgrimage, there must be a deep and irrefutable connection.

THE PASSION AND GREEK TRAGEDY

Bach's Passions may be compared with ancient Greek tragedy; for example, in the use of the chorus. The chorus in the Passion sings: *Sehet* ("Behold"), and five times repeats this call, in the manner of the prophets. And as in the ancient theater the chorus (representing the voice of the people, as contrasted with the actual carriers of the dramatic action) "solemnly treads before and under the stage, enunciating ethical and religious comments," so in the Passion the chorus plays a prophetic role. It follows the action with close attention and supplements it with utterances of questions, answers, observations, and laments on behalf of the congregation which so deeply experiences the mystery of the Saviour's sacrifice that it becomes mystically united with Him.

In the first stages of the ancient drama the solo singer, apart from the chorus, recited the history of the god Dionysos, but was soon joined by other soloists coming from the chorus. Here we see how the sacred drama grew out of a cult dialogue. In Bach's St. Matthew Passion we find that the chorus is divided into two parts (Chorus I and II) from which arise the voices of the Evangelist, Jesus, and the other participants in the life of the Saviour.

Bach's Passion is a spiritual vision, a mystery transformed into music; as such it marks the culmination of musical mysticism. It is at the same time the strongest demonstration of Lutheranism since the lifetime of the great Reformer.

The mystic finds God within himself, in the innermost depth of his soul, apart from everything sensual and earthly. Therefore the supreme representation of the divine must needs be spiritual and visionary. When the great poet and thinker Jean Paul in his vision, *Dreams from the Battlefield,* describes the sphere of bliss in paradise, Christ appears as "the voice without a form." This is the same vision we meet with in the Passion. And this is indeed the last and greatest significance of music, that it expresses Christian mysticism as a vision of tones.

DEVELOPMENT OF THE PASSION

Let us now summarize this development. For centuries it was customary in the Roman Church to read the Passion of Christ from the Gospels on certain days during Holy Week. Three priests alternated in the recitation: the words of Christ were chanted by a deep voice, the narration of the Evangelists by a middle, and all other persons (*soliloquents*), including the disciples, Jews, high priests, and soldiers, by a tenor voice. Plain chanting in simple melodious form characterized this performance. The melodies of the different parts of the Passion, the continued recitation tone, and the flourishes for the beginning of a phrase, the period, comma, colon, question mark, and so on, were accurately laid down. Christ's part was executed in slow solemn measure, the

Evangelist's in a normal tempo, and the crowd's in rapid impassioned measure. In the old manuscripts the part of Christ is marked "T" (*tarde*, slow), that of the Evangelist "C" (*celeriter*, rapid), and that of the people "S" (*sursum*, high). Later we find the sign ✠ for Christ, "C" for the chronicler, "S" (synagogue) for the multitude.

Already in pre-Lutheran days attempts had been made to enrich these performances by musical additions, for instance, by letting the chorus take the role of the crowd. But the chanting of the lesson was nevertheless strictly observed.

In this form the Passion was known to Luther; we shall call it "Chorale Passion" or "Plain Song Passion." Before Luther, parts of the Passion recitations were taken from all four Gospels, but Luther now ordered a limitation to one or two at the most. Since that time the Passion has more often been sung according to one Evangelist (St. Matthew, St. John, St. Mark, and St. Luke). Before Luther, the "Passion Harmony" by Johann Bugenhagen had been used, and for a long time the Reformer sanctioned this version. But it was the Passion after St. Matthew by Johann Walther which was to become the prototype of the Protestant Passion. We know that Walther, together with Konrad Rupsch, had been called to Wittenberg to arrange the music of the German Mass. Walther proceeded to revise the Passion music as well, this entirely according to the Reformer's wishes. The textual basis was Luther's translation of the

Gospel, and Walther followed Luther's suggestion that
German church music should grow out of the very spirit
of the language. W. Lott, in his essay, "History of the
Passion Composition," claims that Walther's Chorale
Passion seems dry compared with other works of the
same time and class. That may be true from the standpoint of music, but surely not when we regard its sincerity from the theological viewpoint. Each musical
accent, each rise and fall of the voice, each emotion of
the speaker, musically presents the sequence of events.
The parts of the crowd are simple and so set harmonically
as to make it easy for almost anyone to sing.

THE FIGURAL PASSION

This "Plain Song Passion" held its position until well
into the seventeenth century. But a new Passion, the so-
called "Figural Passion" (polyphonic), now made its
appearance. The entire text is composed in motet form
for several voices. No difference is made between the
single persons and the chorus.

The Netherlander Obrecht had already cultivated this
form, as had also composers like Balthasar Resinarius,
Joachim von Burgk, Leonhard Lechner, and Christoph
Demantius. Between these two types of the Passion there
was a third which greatly influenced its future development. Chanting was restricted to the part of the Evangelist while the parts of the other persons were composed
in the motet form for several voices. Thus Scandellus
gives to Jesus a four-voiced part; to the maid, Peter, and

Pilate, three-voiced parts; and has the crowd's sung in five-voiced parts.

It is in conformity with the idea of the "Mystery" that a single part should be represented by more than one voice, for thus, musically speaking, a disembodiment, a dissolution of the individual takes place. It would seem as though the composer dared not let Christ and the witnesses of his pilgrimage on earth be sung by one person only — that is, in purely human fashion. In employing this collective form he comes nearer to the idea of the "Mystery."

THE PASSIONS OF SCHUTZ

In the "History of the Joyous and Triumphant Resurrection" (1623) by Heinrich Schütz, the Evangelist sings solo. Jesus' words, however, are sung by a duet of tenor and alto. What a wonderful idea thus to characterize the transfigured Christ! Mary Magdalene is performed by two sopranos in duet form, the youth at the grave by two solo altos. Incidentally, it is stated in the preface that the imitating accompanying voice can, at will, be executed instrumentally. The introduction and the crowds are in six voices, and the conclusion even in nine voices, in which the Evangelist jubilantly joins singing a "Victoria," four times repeated.

Schütz used the old accents of the German Mass as they had been laid down by Luther and Walther. He blended them, however, with the recitation tone of the Florentine monodists as found in the first operas. This is also evident in the score (figured bass in mensural notes, over which the Evangelist-voice is notated in neumes).

The most important and best-known Passions of Schütz are those according to St. Matthew, St. John, and St. Luke, already mentioned. By the simplest means, without either instruments or the figured bass, Schütz arrives at a mystic meditation and a representation of the agony of Christ that, in its way, has never been equaled, not even by Bach. He strives to interpret not only the text but even the differing characters of the Evangelists (at least St. John and St. Matthew). "Intense agitation at the eternal idea of death and resurrection, finding highest expression in the Passion of Christ, emanates from these brief phrases. These Passions are the most dramatic liturgical works in their field. Yet they are not music for the congregation, but the almost unapproachable grandiose art of one who has grown far above society and church" (Blume).

Bach represents an entirely different type of the Passion. His is the contemplative Passion in its philosophical views influenced by pietism. A new feature is devout meditation on the narratives of the Scripture. Allegoric personages (Faith, Truth, etc.), in a free lyrical manner meditate on the events of the passion of Christ as narrated in the Bible, and the congregation participates in this meditation by the singing of hymns. The first exponent of this class is Thomas Strutius of Danzig (who wrote lyrical poems and chorales of a contemplative nature, partly for solo, partly for choir and the congregation, and organized them into acts like those of a drama). The text, but not the music, is still extant. The text, taken word for word from the Gospel of St. Matthew, is in five acts and interspersed with songs. The Passion is framed by chorales. As far as we know, this Passion is the earliest to carry out the new principle of meditation.

TEXTS OF THE PASSION

Compositions before Bach's time are partly based on texts by Christian Friedrich Hunold, who lived in Hamburg. He is known for his opera texts, published under the name of Menantes. His "Bleeding and Dying Jesus" is quite theatrical in structure. The biblical text is entirely eliminated, and the Evangelist and the chorale too have disappeared. The prominent composer Reinhard Keiser wrote the music to this text. We do not know the music but the text is coarsely sensual. He revels in gruesome and at the same time morbidly sweet pictures and thoughts; he wavers, as Arnold Schering in his *History of the Oratorio* has it, "between a coarse realism and symbolic mysticism." In order to understand the spiritual background of this work, we have only to remember the materialistic, sensational, blood-curdling operas which at that time were in vogue in Hamburg. Even Handel came under this influence. But we must also point out a parallel between the Passion of Hunold and the poems of Zinzendorf.

The Hamburg councilor, Barthold Heinrich Brockes,

published a Passion called "Jesus Martyred and Dying for the Sins of the World" (1712), which indicates the next stage in the history of the Passion. The Evangelist is again introduced, but instead of the actual text of the Gospel, Brockes paraphrases it. He does not change the style of Hunold in its essentials; his text contains free recitatives, *da capo* arias, and he again inserts chorale verses. Brockes' libretto was used by masters such as Handel, Telemann, Matheson, and Stölzel. His work was very popular. Since the feeling for language was not so refined as it is in our day, the vulgarities of Brockes' text were hardly noticed by his contemporaries who saw only the dramatic power and the pictorial richness of the text.

Even Bach used this text for his Passion of St. John (but only in parts) for some of the arias which he put to music. The bombastic narration of the Passion in verse he replaced by the words of the Gospel. This is significant. For while many of his contemporaries saw in Brockes a poetic genius, the orthodox Lutheran, Bach, reverted to the original text of the Gospel. More than that: as in the Passions of Schütz so also here the individual character of the Gospels is expressed in music. His musical language is wonderfully adapted to the specific spirit of the narrative of the Gospel. He is therefore the interpreter of the Gospel *kat' exochen* — an interpreter whose device, "The Word they still shall let remain," has here borne marvelous fruit.

St. John and St. Matthew

New Testament scholars believe that the fourth Gospel was written several decades after the others. In the foreground of this Gospel is not the material collected for a presentation of the life of Jesus, but His life as viewed by the Christian congregation of that day. And therefore this Evangelist, as one who has seen and known the Lord, speaks with the authority of a witness to this great drama. This explains the dramatic emphasis on those events in which Christ appears more as the ruler of the world than as the gentle benign "friend of the soul," of pietist conception of that day.

The Passion of St. John puts special emphasis on the great judgment scenes before the High Priest and Pilate. They are pervaded by an impassioned, agitated spirit, and Bach has seized this mood when he makes the priest-and-people choruses the carriers of the action.

The St. Matthew Passion is differently conceived. This is the story of the Passion closest to Bach's heart. It is more tender, more human, more consoling. It depicts Jesus as Bach saw Him and loved Him. How fundamentally different is the treatment of the narrative by the Evangelists in these two Gospels. The narration in the St. Matthew Passion begins in the "Jesus key" (G major), calm and mild as though Bach were speaking of a dear friend; and the voice of Jesus himself seems embedded in soft sound of the string orchestra around which float the words of the Lord like an aureole, a halo. Christ is represented as both human and divine.

How unlike the Passion of St. John, in which the Gospel words are characterized in C minor, and the accents, sharply dramatic, follow in strong beats. Great and omnipotent, the voice of a world ruler, the words of Jesus ring out. In the same manner do the choruses of the two Passions differ. The chorus "Crucify" is a violent outburst of the crowds, while in the St. Matthew Passion it is solemn and weighty — a vision of Christ carrying His cross.

Whereas the St. John Passion concentrates on the narrative of the Evangelist emphasizing the cruelty and tragedy of the judgment and death of the Lord, the Passion of St. Matthew stresses the thought of redemption by the death of Christ. This accounts for the large number of arias and choruses, which leaves wide room for emotions and serves to further a mood of mystic contemplation.

LUTHERANISM IN BACH'S PASSIONS

Thus, in the St. John and St. Matthew Passions, the two phases of Lutheranism of that age are represented. In the Passion of St. John it is orthodoxy, and in the St. Matthew Passion, pietism, which is typified. In the former it is the idea of law, the word, and its fulfillment before which man helplessly is left to the mercy of God; in the latter it is the grace of God which finds sounding expression in Bach's music. The joy and confidence of the believer that grew out of the events at Golgotha cause him, in his bliss, his glowing joy, to descend to the very depths of his soul, where he in reverential awe divines the mystery of his being and its union with God and the world. This union of the ego with the Godhead and living nature is, it would seem, the profound secret of the Passion. It would not at first sight appear that this work reflects the living creation of God, for no bird's voice, no flower, no rustling of the forest reverberates in it. And yet this music is that of the eternal cosmos, of almighty nature. Christ, the Lord, the Man, dies — so that millions shall live. He dies at a time when the world renews itself, when plants and animals are regenerated. Death and transfiguration, sin and forgiveness, hate and reconciliation — these are the basic pillars of this music. And it is thus that we must interpret the celestial sound of the final chorus *Ruhe sanfte, sanfte Ruh'*. We here feel, after deep sorrow and meditation, that the light of the sun and the verdure of spring are hailing us. . . .

Perhaps Bach's Passions are the most magnificent exponents of Lutheranism and Protestantism. It is in this spirit that Dilthey says: "The aim of faith and religion as such is, according to Luther, the joyous feeling of a divine providence, brought about by justification, which is the moral possession, and therefore the blessedness, of life itself."

These words give best evidence of the connection between Luther and Bach. They tell us why Luther is bound up with the modern development of music as no other nonmusician.

CHAPTER SIX

LUTHER AND BACH

Bach was a deeply devout, convinced follower of Luther. A number of theological works were found after his death, and among them was a complete edition of Luther's works. From the polemic literature also represented it is evident that the great master adhered strictly to Lutheran views. In Cöthen his children were to attend the Reformed school, but Bach sent them to the newly founded Lutheran school for instruction. His attitude toward pietism was antagonistic. Spitta very exhaustively describes the confusion reigning in church matters in Mühlhausen, where Bach was the organist of St. Blasius, 1707-08. Feeling ran high between the pietist and the orthodox parties, and pastors carried the controversy even into the pulpits. Bach's superior, Johann Adolph Frohne, pastor of St. Mary's, was the leader of the pietists, while Georg Christian Eilmar was the head of the orthodox believers. According to Spitta, Frohne was a man of deep religious feeling, of undoubted moral rectitude and rigorous severity toward himself as well as toward others. He demanded both good works and repentance and was therefore accused of pietism by a large part of his congregation. Eilmar, on the other hand, was the typical representative of orthodoxy, without a trace of warm religious feeling, but characterized by a loquacious presumptuousness and aggressive rudeness. He was, in fact, the typical dogmatic theologian. And yet we see Bach on the side of the orthodox pedant and schoolmaster. He must have been very close to Eilmar, in spite of the fact that Eilmar was the opponent of his superior — which again is evidence of the sincerity of the master. Eilmar was godfather to Bach's first child — an honor accorded only to the intimates of his household — and one of his greatest cantatas, *Aus der Tiefe rufe ich Herr,* bears the notation: "By request of Tit. Herren Georg Christ. Eilmar, put into music by Joh. Seb. Bach, Org. Molhusino."

BACH, THE LUTHERAN

How is Bach's attitude to be explained? He had been brought up in the tradition of strict Lutheran belief. For generations the Bachs had been devout Lutherans. And Sebastian's education, under the direction of an older brother at the orthodox Lyceum at Ohrdruf, was not of a nature to have caused any change in this strict tradition; moreover, in Arnstadt, the scene of his activities as an organist, he found himself in a rigidly orthodox atmosphere. The pietistic ideas must have been contrary to his strong straightforward nature, his single-mindedness, and, last but not least, to his philosophy as a musician. For pietism undoubtedly brought about a relaxation of the inner stability of man, a weakening of the

manly, intransigent attitude of the old Protestantism, nor
could the maudlin sentimentalism of pietism appeal to a
character like that of Bach. All the more so since this
theological doctrine had aimed to ban music as an art
from all the churches — quite contrary to the Lutheran
idea that music in its artistic development was an "instrument of the Holy Spirit." And yet pietism has left deep
traces in the works of Bach. It again goes to show that
the inner life of a genius has little to do with his outer
life. Theoretically, Bach refused to accept pietism, but
his works were imbued with the spirit of mysticism and
pietism. In the last analysis, is not his musical symbolism,
his tone painting, a phenomenon running parallel with
the pietistic Jesus phantasies?

When in 1722 Bach accepted the position of musical
director of the St. Thomas Cantorate and the University
of Leipzig, which he held until his death in 1750, he was
obliged to sign the venerable Formula of Concord. This
was the last symbolic document of Lutheranism, stem-
ming from the sixteenth century, which was designed to
unite all the Lutheran churches of Germany.

This confession had put an end to all theological dis-
putes. It refuted not only Calvinism but also the milder
form of Lutheranism as introduced by Melanchthon.
Bach could sign this formula without scruples, for such
a Christian was he that Dr. Martin Luther himself could
have desired none better.

In his *Thorough Instruction in the Figured Bass*, which
he dedicated to his pupils, Bach assimilated Luther's ideas.

We seem to hear a paraphrase of one of Luther's Table Talks, when we read the second chapter of this instruction: "The figured bass is the most perfect fundamental of music. Played with both hands, it is so executed that the left hand plays the prescribed notes, while the right accompanies with con- and dis-sonances. Thus a tuneful harmony is achieved to the glory of God, and for an admissible delectation of the soul. It should, like all music, have as its sole aim the glory of God and the recreation of the soul. Where this rule is not observed there is no real music, but only a devilish blubbering and whining." In a booklet of organ music he adds the following verse:

> *Dem höchsten Gott allein zu Ehren*
> *Dem Nächsten draus sich zu belehren.*
>
> For the glory of God on high
> And the improvement of my fellow-man.

A Service in Leipzig

Luther's principle, "Edification and Education," is here very obvious. And in the *Klavier Büchlein*, written for his first-born son, Friedemann, we find the notation: *In nomine Jesu* ("In the name of Jesus"). The most decisive years of Bach's life were passed in Leipzig. St. Thomas' Church was the scene of the greater part of his activities; and since earlier in this book we considered a service in the Lutheran Church of the sixteenth century, so now, by way of comparison, a description of a service in St. Thomas' Church may be of interest.

The service began at seven o'clock. After the playing of the organ came the motet, the Introit followed, and after that the Kyrie was sung first in German, then in Latin. The Gloria was intoned from the altar, whereupon either the choir responded with "and on earth, peace" or the congregation with "all glory be to God on high." After the collect the Epistle was chanted. A hymn of the congregation was added, whereupon the Gospel was chanted by the pastor, who also intoned the Creed. The organist now improvised a prelude, but confined himself to the key notes needed by the instruments to tune in. At a signal from the cantor he stopped. The cantata now began and at the end the hymn, "We all believe in one true God," was sung.

The cantata lasted at most twenty minutes. This limit of time was observed especially in winter, for, should the performance be too long, there was danger that both performers and congregation might suffer from the severe Leipzig weather. It was no small matter to remain in an unheated church for three or four hours. As a rule, the St. Thomas chorus singers went to the near-by school to warm themselves during the sermon. But even there it was obligatory that a sermon be given. After the sermon in church came prayer and blessing, then a chorale introducing the second part of the divine service, the Holy Communion. During communion hymns were sung in the German language, and it was then that Bach must have played the organ. His preludes to communion hymns give eloquent proof of this. Organ preludes and church cantatas (Bach, following the old custom, called them "church concertos") were the forms in which the great cantor served his Creator. In these musical forms he expressed his own faith and that of his fellow-believers. His organ music, based on the church chorale and easily accessible to the congregation, but nevertheless on the highest spiritual level, reflects the religious spirit of his age. It is fundamentally of an orthodox nature, but it also expresses the pietistic feeling and striving for an inner spirituality. It submerges itself in the content of the Word of the chorale and reveals the woes of the Passion. All the ecstasies of the sweet love of the Saviour, as well as the yearning for a union of the soul with Christ, are expressed in these chorales. And here is indeed the deeper sense of Bach's music: the union of the revealed Word of God (as symbolized in the chorale) with man's emotional response to this Word. It is the synthesis of orthodoxy and pietism — these two tendencies which so bitterly opposed each other, in writing and from the pulpit, but which blossomed forth in Bach's music in such wondrous beauty and unity.

The "Actus Tragicus"

Bach wrote about three hundred church cantatas, of which two-thirds have been preserved. His early cantatas, for example the *Actus Tragicus*, were written in the old form called *Spruch Cantata*. Bach himself collected this text from the Bible quotations, and it can be called one of the most perfect of all the cantatas by this

master. Bach later adopted the new form (introduced
by Erdmann Neumeister and the well-known librettist,
Brockes), as in the *Erbauungs Cantata* ("Edification Cantata") — with free paraphrasing of Bible texts in the form
of simple recitative and aria — while in the old form he
had applied the arioso, which is more personal and less
formal than the aria taken over from the opera. In the
newer cantata, the choir is more or less eliminated, and
it was only later (1711) that Bach again included the
chorale and the biblical word.

The inclusion of the aria in the cantata was denounced
by the pietists as being too operatic and unchurchly. But
the introduction of this style is entirely in line with
Bach's orthodox Lutheran philosophy, which takes the
point of view that all forms of music which served the
musician's purpose could and should be embraced in the
church service.

While Bach, in this respect, follows the orthodox
Lutheran principles, the emotional content of his cantatas
is in many cases mystic and pietistic. Schweitzer goes so
far as to claim that Bach in his innermost being was the
manifestation of German mysticism: "This strong man,
who in his family life and in his activities stood firmly
in the midst of life and the world, and on whose face
is seen something of the pleasure of life, was in his innermost soul dead to the world. His whole being was
transfigured by a wonderful, happy yearning for death."
It is true that mystic thoughts pervade many of his cantatas; it is also true that never in his music is he more

moving than when he preaches the deliverance of the soul
from the body. Let us take, as an example, his *Actus
Tragicus*, which, according to Pirro, was written as early
as 1707 on the death of his uncle, Lämmerhirt, and which
is infused with a fervor, a personal tenderness, which
Bach has attained in no other of his later works. The
introductory sonatina projects us into the mood that
overcomes the true believer at the approach of death.
Dark mysterious tones take us into the valley of the
shadow of death which has nothing terrifying in it, but
is sweet and appeasing. The basses move in firm inexorable step yet with calm and painless measure. They speak
of eternal divine reconciliation. Over them play the
somber gambas and lamenting flutes, while the descend-
ing fifths and sixths sound like the sobbing in a moving
dialogue of bidding farewell to the dead. . . . An infinitely
sorrowful yet consoling feeling emanates from these
musical phrases which later — in symbolic and characteristic form — again overcome us at the words, "Today
shalt thou be with me in paradise" and "Come, Lord
Jesus." Bach, then, in the instrumental introduction,
aims to affirm the absolute certainty of the union of the
soul with Christ. One of the greatest tone painters of all
time, he has accomplished this with a realistic percep-
tivity, a fervency, a zeal, that greatly transcend the poetic
outbursts of a Spener or a Zinzendorf.

Having fixed, in the sonatina, the mood of the cantata,
Bach now proceeds to depict the destiny of man in his
relation to God. "God's time is ever best" — an *allegro*

fugato sung by the choir — grips the hearer and arouses in him the resolve to accept with joy God's will. Life passes in rapid chords: "In Him we live and move." But now grandiose, column-like chords announce the approach of death: "In Him we die in His good time." In the words of the Ninetieth Psalm we hear the admonition, "So teach us to number our days." O'er this tenor solo the flute, impassioned and animated, plays a beautiful melody. It is the interpretation of the psalm, speaking of solace and the promise of paradise. Now, with great suddenness, sounds the admonition of death, "Set thine house in order" (Isa. 38:1), which like a gale rushes over the autumn field, blowing away all thoughts of earthly trifles. . . . Now we hear the stern inexorable word paraphrased from the Old Testament: "It is the ancient law; man, thou must die," symbolized by a fugue. But immediately upon this, we have a tender and simple soprano melody, "Even so, come, Lord Jesus." This points to the Gospel with its doctrine of the salvation of man by Christ, which is above the Old Testament. Hardly has this melody (a symbolic and trusting message), died away when we hear, executed by the instruments, another melody. The flute, accompanied by the violas, with almost celestial beauty, plays the chorale, "I have committed all to God." This is the symbol of salvation by grace. Bach here shows how the grace of God is above all earthly things, even above the good works flowing from personal faith, thus announcing Luther's message of justification. The instruments die away, one after another. The world is gradually falling away from the dying, and in a tender, confident prayer, "Come Lord Jesus," on the irrevocable, inexorable pedal point of "F," the phrase ends. Its breath-taking close seems to project us into eternity. . . . Out of it rises the duet, "Into thy hands I commend my spirit." The dying thief (alto) now enters on a dialogue with Jesus (bass) himself, who answers, "Today shalt thou be with me in paradise." And while the violas are painting the beauties of paradise, the old Luther chorale is heard *Mit Fried und Freud fahr ich dahin* ("In peace and joy I pass away"), sung by the alto. We hear floating on high the sobbing phrases of the sonatina that speak of both sadness and bliss and with supreme divination give us a glimpse of paradise.

No mortal before or after Bach has been able to bring this about in so breath-taking a manner. Here the master penetrates into the innermost depths of mysticism — deeper than all the mystics of word and thought — and unfolds for us the secret of the individual and his death. And now that the mystery has been unfolded, the curtain falls. Now follow, first the Creed set to the symbolic melody, "In Thee had I hoped," and then the grandiose closing chorus, "All Glory, Praise, and Majesty." All this is indeed the quintessence of the Lutheran belief, the artistic transfiguration of the Reformer's doctrine.

In order to show how Luther and his doctrine live in the music of Bach, we would have to analyze all his cantatas. This is a task which will occupy musicological research for decades to come.

THE REFORMATION CANTATA

We cannot close this chapter on Luther and Bach without referring to his great *Reformation Cantata*, "A Mighty Fortress is Our God," for it plainly reveals how Bach's orthodox Lutheran belief is blended with the pietistic adoration of Jesus.

We have already spoken of the connection of Bach's cantatas with the various Sundays and Festivals of the Church Year. As Psalm 46 had been prescribed for the Reformation Festival, so the hymn *Ein' feste Burg* was also designated for this day.

We do not know in what year Bach composed this cantata. Spitta thinks that 1730 might be the answer, since at that time the Reformation celebration was held with special pomp. He also believes that 1739, the two hundredth jubilee anniversary in Saxony, might possibly have been the occasion for which it was written.

In the composition of this work Bach took over parts of an earlier cantata that was written for Oculi Sunday and supplemented these with the two gigantic choruses from Luther's battle song: the beginning, "A mighty Fortress," and the line, "Though devils all the world should fill." Luther's melody forms the solid framework of the cantata, and the variations and the interpretations of it are of unusual structure. What unheard-of expressions! When "the old bitter foe" appears, Luther's simple but intensely pictorial melody mounts to an anguished uncanny effect; it is as though the heavenly legions were intoning this battle song against the archenemy. This Michelangelesque effect is again surpassed when suddenly Luther's chorale, in its original form, is sounded by the trumpets and oboes from on high. And, as if all this were not enough for the glory of God, Bach again lets ring out "A mighty Fortress" from the basses and the organ basses and they, together with the trumpets, carry out the canon. This is a jubilation and glorification of the Lord, and the sun and the stars with their harmony of the spheres seem to join in the *cantus firmus* "A mighty Fortress" — the one fixed point around which the universe turns. We stand transfixed with wonder at this phenomenon — how faith, transformed here into a divine work of genius, could accomplish this miracle of the human spirit.

The second stanza, "With might of ours can naught be done," is composed as a duet. The soprano sings the lines of the verse in light figuration, accompanied by the oboe and strings. The bass now begins in weighty measure: "Every soul by God created has by Christ been liberated," and then *"Wer bei Christi Blut Panier in der Taufe treu geschworen, siegt im Geiste fuer und fuer"* ("They who Jesus' standard bear, to His service dedicated, all will in His vict'ry share") — a text from the Epistle for Quasi Modo Geniti Sunday, the so-called "White Sunday" (I John 5:4-12). That was an old baptismal date, on which heathen were baptized in white gowns.

As man by baptism is born to new life (so teaches Bach) he shall be reborn in spirit by the doctrine of the Reformation, the Gospel. Now follow the recitative, arioso, and aria, which in pietistic manner express love to Jesus. "Come, dwell within my heart, Lord Jesus, I adore Thee; out, sin, how base thou art . . ." sings the soprano in sweet melody. Then suddenly follows a violent battle music, performed by the orchestra, to which the choir in piercing unison sings: "Though devils all the world should fill." This depicts the battle of the cherubim against Satan, the jubilant victorious symphony of the good spirits over evil. Again we hear the pietistic recitative, "So take thy stand with Christ," which is followed by the arioso, "Salvation now is sure," a piece overflowing with sweet and tender devotion. The text is from the Epistle to the Romans (10:9-13). After the singing of this chorale by the congregation, accompanied by the organ only, the following "The Word they still shall let remain" is a powerful and triumphant consummation. It is the firm unshaken avowal of the optimism pervading a soul which has deeply experienced the miracle of grace and the joy in the creative power of God, as has Johann Sebastian Bach.

This optimism, based on a firm trust in God, on the belief in the grace of God, breathes in all of Bach's works, his cantatas no less than in his fugues and toccatas, his sonatas, and suites. They give voice not only to his own philosophy but that of his age, of which he is the musical exponent. And as his spiritual point of view is felt in every harmony, in every rhythmic and melodic phrase, his music also expresses the standpoint of the thinkers, poets, politicians, and burghers of that period. Bach's age has been thoughtlessly called the age of absolutism — defining it as one which lacked freedom of thought. One recalls how an artist or a scholar, in the pay of a prince, had to serve him and be at his will and command. As if a genius soaring far above time and space could be fettered by any command, court etiquette, or fashion!

PHILOSOPHY AND MUSIC

If we wish to have an insight into the spiritual or intellectual workshop of an artist, it will be well to regard not only his tools — in this case the musical technique — but the parallel forces of the mind and soul in the field of philosophy, which, like all art, are the intellectual expression of an age. Just as Wagner and Schopenhauer, Beethoven and Kant, belong together, so are Bach and Leibnitz (the greatest and clearest thinker at the turn of the eighteenth century) of one mind.

The world of nature, according to Leibnitz, consists of numberless small soul units called "monads." Each monad carries within itself the entire harmonious world picture, in darker or clearer representation, in the ratio of the progress made in the striving for perfect perception of the whole. The degree of clarity reached determines the order of arrangement of the monads to one another. Those monads which have attained the clearest perception after striving become leader monads. Thus does the soul become leader of the body, the monarch leader of the state, and thus is the universe as a whole built up from the smallest unit to the all-embracing whole: a unified entity, harmonious and centralized, which is God. This world system is borne along by a harmonious, ceaselessly flowing divine power, which manifests itself in every unit, even the individual, but not as something that is special to himself, as a personal will-directed action, but as fate, as grace, as the divine world-stream power that actuates the All.

And this surely is not the mental picture corresponding to a political absolutism. It is rather the picture of a close union, the picture of an everlasting life together — it is true, under the protection and direction of a higher law, that is, religion.

And this is exactly what Bach's music proclaims to us: the uninterrupted course of the world is symbolized in ever-weaving monads (motifs) with their melodies, which, like the wheel of the divine Providence, rotate, and which rest on the figured bass: the fundament of faith.

In contrast to the later classical music of Haydn, Mozart, and Beethoven, whose fundamental form was that of the bithematic sonata, the music of Bach and his contemporaries is monothematic. And the monothematic fugue — with its rigid structure the basis of which is the fifth, with its strictly regulated possibilities of variations, with its enlargements and abbreviations of the theme, with its development, exposition, and coda — is the tonal reflection of the Leibnitz doctrine of monads. The Bach student, Mizler, made the following observation: "Music is, so to say, the mirror of the changes possible in the world. But the fact that music has, next to theology, a specially high mission in the divine order of the world has often been pointed out by Luther."

It is in the theories of Leibnitz that we find embodied the life of the people of that time: freedom of personality and freedom of will — within the limit of the law (which was the doctrine of Luther). The burgher experienced the pre-established harmony through religion alone. He understood the world as the creation of God, under the authority of the Church, within which he could allow his own personality to develop. For him not even the idea of time passed into the uncertain. He lived in the order of the Church Year, and each day had its meaning in the sense of the Gospel — with an outlook into eternity. Everything: religion, family, state, and the individual being, derived its law from God.

There is a deep significance in the fact that Bach's activities fell in a period when Luther's doctrine was in its latest bloom of orthodoxy and pietism. When, in the later period, life and religion were secularized, a secularization of music resulted. With the now ever-growing emphasis on the personality, and a receding from the law, a period of estrangement to Luther's doctrine necessarily set in. A psychological treatment of music was the result. An exaggerated elevation of individual personality followed, which found expression in the church music of the Vienna composers.

With Bach, however, the old Lutheran concept of music had died.

CONCLUSION

At the close of this discussion of Luther and music, the question arises what course the development and history of music would have taken, had not Luther, but Calvin, prevailed in the Reformation of Germany. Could we possibly conceive of a history of music without the class of greater and lesser organists and cantors from which rose the generation of the Bachs and of Handel, the generation of Praetorius, Schein, Scheidt, and Schütz? And to whom belonged Demantius, Hammerschmidt, Kuhnau, Telemann, Buxtehude, Tunder, Ahle, Rist, Crüger, and a host of others — building stones of that monumental edifice of German music in the seventeenth and eighteenth centuries?

Let us compare with this the fields of Calvinist Reformation, for instance, Switzerland and Holland — countries which have contributed little to the development of music in the past centuries. The contribution of Calvinism to the development of music in France was comparatively small. In that country music began to flourish anew from the middle of the seventeenth century on, when Italian and Catholic influence became more prevalent. The development of English music, from the seventeenth century on, is another example. And let us remember that the Calvinistic doctrine allowed the hymn a very modest role in its liturgy.

From Luther, however, emanated a steadily growing stream, not only of faith in God and of moral consciousness, but also of a joy in living and with it a profoundly mystic experience of God, which is based on the universal and direct priesthood, the doctrine of justification and of Christian freedom. Dilthey sums it up thus: "The religiosity of Lutheranism cannot be fully understood by the dogmatic works alone; for its documents are the writings of Luther, the hymn, the sacred music of Bach and Handel, and the formation of religious life. The distinctive character of this form of religion lies in its vitality, which does not alone, in the religious experience out of the fullness of the human power, raise the moral will to a union with the Godhead and make the life of man a service to God — but in a profound feeling of life from which emanates indivisibility that brings it into affinity with the highest."

BIBLIOGRAPHY

BACHMANN, FRANZ. *Grundlagen und Grundfragen zur evangelischen Kirchenmusik.* Gütersloh, Bertelsmann. 1899.

BERGER, A. E. *Martin Luther in Kulturgeschichtlicher Darstellung.* Berlin, Hoffman. 1895-1921.

BESSELER, HEINRICH. *Die Musik des Mittelalters und der Renaissance.* Potsdam, Akad. Verlags. Athenaion. 1931.

BLUME, FRIEDRICH. *Das monodische Prinzip in der evangelischen Kirchenmusik.* Potsdam, Akad. Verlags. Athenaion. 1925.

BLUME, FRIEDRICH. *Die evangelische Kirchenmusik.* Potsdam, Akad. Verlags. Athenaion. 1931.

BUKOFZER, MANFRED. *Music in the Baroque Era; from Monteverdi to Bach.* New York, Norton. 1947.

BUSZIN, WALTER E. *Luther on Music* in *Musical Quarterly*, January, 1946. New York.

DAVISON, ARCHIBALD T. *Protestant Church Music in America.* Boston, Schirmer. 1933.

DICKINSON, EDWARD. *Music in the History of the Western Church.* New York, Scribner. 1925.

DILTHEY, WILHELM. *Gesammelte Schriften.* 12 vols. Berlin, Teubner. 1922-36.

DILTHEY, WILHELM. *Von deutscher Dichtung und Musik.* Leipzig, Teubner. 1933.

DOUGLAS, WINFRED. *Church Music in History and Practice.* New York, Scribner. 1940.

GEBHARDT, FRANZ. *Die musikalische Grundlage zu Luthers deutscher Messe.* Gütersloh, Bertelsmann. 1930.

GERBER, RUDOLF. *Die deutsche Passion von Luther bis Bach* in *Luther Jahrbuch.* Munich, Luthergesellschaft. 1931.

GERBER, RUDOLF. *Zu Luthers Liedweisen* in *Festschrift Max Schneiders...* Eisleben-Lutherstadt. 1935.

GROVE, GEORGE (ED.). *Dictionary of Music and Musicians, 1450-1880.* 3rd ed. 6 vols. New York, Scribner. 1939.

HAAS, ROBERT M. *Musik des Barocks.* Potsdam, Akad. Verlags. Athenaion. 1928.

The Heritage of the Church in *Proceedings of the Institute of Religious Music.* University Press, Valparaiso. 1946-47.

HERZ, GERHARD. *Bach's Religion* in *Journal of Renaissance and Baroque Music,* March, 1946. Cambridge.

JULIAN, JOHN (ED.). *Dictionary of Hymnology.* Rev. ed. London, Murray. 1925.

KADE, OTTO. *Die ältere Passionskomposition bis zum Jahre 1631.* Gütersloh, Bertelsmann. 1893.

KRETZSCHMAR, HERMANN. *Luther und die Musik* in *Jahrbuch der Musikbibliothek Peters.* Leipzig. 1917.

LANG, PAUL H. *Music in Western Civilization.* New York, Norton. 1941.

LEICHTENTRITT, HUGO. *Geschichte der Motette.* Leipzig, Breitkopf und Härtel. 1908.

LOTT, WALTER. *Zur Geschichte der Passions-komposition* in *Archiv für Musikwissenschaft* III and VII. Leipzig. 1920 and 1925.

LUTHER, MARTIN. *Musikalische Schriften* in *Werke; kritisch gesamtausgabe.* 57 vols. Weimar und Leipzig. 1883——. *Die Singweisen* in vol. 35.

MOSER, HANS J. *Die evangelische Kirchenmusik im volkstümlicher Ueberblick.* Stuttgart, Engelhorns. 1926.

Moser, Hans J. *Die Melodien der Lutherlieder* in *Welt des Gesangbuchs*. Leipzig, Schloessmann. 1935.

Moser, Hans J. *Der Zerbster Lutherfund* in *Archiv für Musikwissenschaft* II. Leipzig. 1919.

Moser, Hans J. *Geschichte der deutschen Musik*. 2 vols. Stuttgart, Cotta. 1920.

Phillips, C. S. *Hymnody Past and Present*. London, S.P.C.K. 1937.

Pratt, Waldo S. *The History of Music*. Rev. ed. New York, Schirmer. 1930.

Preuss, Hans. *Martin Luther der Künstler*. Gütersloh, Bertelsmann. 1931.

Ranke, Leopold von. *Deutsche Geschichte im Zeitalter der Reformation* in *Sammtliche Werke*. Bde 1-6. Leipzig, Duncker. 1873.

Reed, Luther D. *The Lutheran Liturgy*. Philadelphia, Muhlenberg Press. 1947.

Schering, Arnold (Ed.). *Bach Jahrbuch*. Leipzig, Breitkopf und Härtel. 1905-30.

Schering, Arnold. *Evangelische Kirchenmusik* in Guido Adler (Ed.); *Handbuch der Musikgeschichte*. 2 vols. Berlin, Keller. 1930.

Schweitzer, Albert. *J. S. Bach*. Eng. tr. by Ernest Newman. London, Black. 1923.

Spitta, Philip. *J. S. Bach*. Eng. tr. by Clara Bell and J. A. F. Maitland. New York, Gray. 1899.

Steglich, Rudolf. *J. S. Bach*. Potsdam, Akad. Verlags. Athenaion. 1935.

Troeltsch, Ernst. *The Social Teaching of the Christian Churches*. Eng. tr. by Olive Wyon. London, Macmillan. 1931.

Zahn, Johannes. *Die Melodien der deutschen evangelischen Kirchenlieder*. 6 vols. Gütersloh, Bertelsmann. 1889-93.

INDEX